The teachings of China's preeminent philosopher come to life

"Every person has the capacity to embody the Way of Heaven…. The goal is fulfilled through a life of learning, where all life's actions become occasions for reflection and for the understanding of the self. There is no action and no thought that is not part of the learning process."

—from the Introduction

Also Available in the SkyLight Illuminations Series

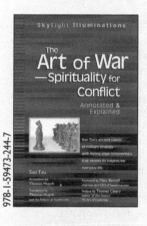

SkyLight Illuminations

The Art of War
—Spirituality for Conflict
Annotated & Explained

Sun Tzu's ancient classic of military strategy—with facing-page commentary that reveals its insights for everyday life.

Sun Tzu

Annotation by Thomas Huynh

Translated by Thomas Huynh and the Editors at Sonshi.com

978-1-59473-244-7

SkyLight Illuminations

Tao Te Ching
Annotated & Explained

An inspiring, precise translation of the ancient Chinese wisdom classic—with facing-page commentary that brings the text to life for you.

Translation and Annotation by Derek Lin

Foreword by Marc Benioff chairman and CEO of Salesforce.com

978-1-59473-204-1

SkyLight Illuminations

Chuang-tzu
The Tao of Perfect Happiness
Selections Annotated & Explained

The wisdom of the foundational Taoist text, with facing-page commentary that brings the text to life.

Translation & Annotation by Livia Kohn author of Health and Long Life The Chinese Way

978-1-59473-296-6

SkyLight Illuminations

Bhagavad Gita
Annotated & Explained

"the very best Gita for first-time readers."

The sacred scripture of India with facing-page commentary that brings the text to life for you.

Translation by Shri Purohit Swami

Annotation by Kendra Crossen Burroughs

Series Editor: Andrew Harvey

978-1-893361-28-7

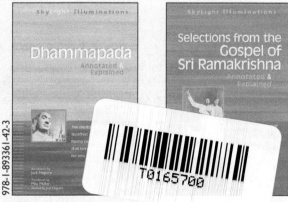

SkyLight Illuminations

Dhammapada
Annotated & Explained

The most beloved Buddhist classic—with facing-page commentary that brings the text to life for you.

Annotation by Jack Maguire

Translated by Max Müller Revised by Jack Maguire

978-1-893361-42-3

Skylight Illuminations

Selections from the Gospel of Sri Ramakrishna
Annotated & Explained

For more information about these and other SkyLight Paths books, please visit our website, www.skylightpaths.com.

T0165700

Rodney L. Taylor, PhD, the foremost American researcher of Confucius as a religious and spiritual figure, is author of *The Religious Dimensions of Confucianism*, *The Way of Heaven*, *The Confucian Way of Contemplation* and *The Illustrated Encyclopedia of Confucianism*, among other books. He is professor of religious studies at the University of Colorado at Boulder, where he also served as director of Asian studies, chair of the Department of Religious Studies and associate dean of the Graduate School.

"The most thoroughly researched and absorbing work of its kind on Confucian and indeed classical Chinese religious, educational, social and ethical thought in general known to me in my more than forty years of college-level teaching in religious studies."
—**Frederick M. Denny,** professor emeritus of religious studies, University of Colorado at Boulder

"A timely and welcome addition to the growing corpus of books that highlight the relevance of Confucianism in the contemporary world.... Unabashedly personal ... with an emphasis on [Confucianism's] religious dimensions."
—**Richard Shek,** professor of humanities and religious studies, California State University, Sacramento

"Becoming morally mature while continuing to learn—what could be more relevant in the world today? Rodney Taylor's [volume] provides an inspiring guide to this goal in a new reading of the Chinese classic that also takes into account its profound practical relevance. A must read!"
—**Livia Kohn,** Boston University; translator and annotator, *Chuang-tzu: The Tao of Perfect Happiness— Selections Annotated & Explained*

Sky Light Illuminations

Offers today's spiritual seeker an enjoyable entry into the great classic texts of the world's spiritual traditions. Each classic is presented in an accessible translation, with facing pages of guided commentary from experts, offering readers the keys they need to understand the history, context and meaning of the text. The series enables readers of all backgrounds to experience and understand classic spiritual texts directly, and to make them a part of their lives.

Walking Together, Finding the Way®

SKYLIGHT PATHS®
PUBLISHING

www.skylightpaths.com

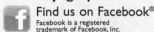

Find us on Facebook®
Facebook is a registered
trademark of Facebook, Inc.

Confucius,
the Analects

Books in the
SkyLight Illuminations Series

Confucius, the Analects

The Path of the Sage

Selections Annotated & Explained

Annotation by Rodney L. Taylor, PhD
Translation by James Legge;
Revised by Rodney L. Taylor, PhD

Walking Together, Finding the Way®
SKYLIGHT PATHS®
PUBLISHING

Confucius, the Analects:
The Path of the Sage—Selections Annotated & Explained

2011 Quality Paperback Edition, First Printing
Introduction, revised translation, and annotations © 2011 by Rodney L. Taylor

Library of Congress Cataloging-in-Publication Data
Confucius.
  [Lun yü. English. Selections]
  Confucius, the analects : the path of the sage : selections annotated & explained / annotation by Rodney L. Taylor ; translation by James Legge ; revised by Rodney L. Taylor. — Quality paperback ed.
      p. cm. — (Skylight illuminations series)
  Includes bibliographical references.
  ISBN 978-1-59473-306-2 (quality pbk.)
  1. Confucius. Lun yu. I. Taylor, Rodney Leon, 1944– II. Legge, James, 1815–1897. III. Title. IV. Title: Path of the sage.
  PL2478.L37 2011
  181'.112—dc22

                                                                                    2011000886

Cover Design: Walter C. Bumford III, Stockton, Massachusetts
Cover Art: Confucius Temple, Shanghai, China © TMAX #3554187 / fotolia.com
Manufactured in the United States of America

SkyLight Paths Publishing is creating a place where people of different spiritual traditions come together for challenge and inspiration, a place where we can help each other understand the mystery that lies at the heart of our existence.

SkyLight Paths sees both believers and seekers as a community that increasingly transcends traditional boundaries of religion and denomination—people wanting to learn from each other, *walking together, finding the way*®.

SkyLight Paths, "Walking Together, Finding the Way" and colophon are trademarks of LongHill Partners, Inc., registered in the U.S. Patent and Trademark Office.

Walking Together, Finding the Way®
Published by SkyLight Paths Publishing
www.skylightpaths.com

ISBN 978-1-68336-013-1 (hc.)

When a parent dies, the child buries the parent in the earth.
When a child dies, the parent buries the child in their heart.

Korean proverb

To the memory of our daughter Meghan (1978–2003)

Contents

Introduction □

A Living Tradition

A number of years ago, as a young scholar, I studied in Kyoto, Japan. My field of research then as now was Confucianism. As my time in Japan unfolded, I was engaged in translating a work of Okada Takehiko, a professor at Kyushu University and a great scholar of Confucianism, from Japanese. I wrote to him to ask for clarification of certain sections of his work, and he invited me and my wife to come visit him in Fukuoka, far from Kyoto on the southern island of Kyushu.

My first meeting with Okada Takehiko was remarkable, as were the subsequent years of interaction between us. He had come to the train station to meet us. As we rode together in the taxi to our hotel he turned to me and said that he believed the world was in profound moral decline and then asked me what we could do about it! This was not an abstract scholarly question, but a plea from a heart and mind that felt the disarray of the contemporary world caught without a moral rudder to bring it back on course.

Through our relationship, I came to understand that Confucianism is not a historical relic of a philosophical value system, but a living tradition of great religious and spiritual depth. The teaching of Confucianism can be summarized, as Okada explained to me, by suggesting that we must turn to live with the moral goodness inherent within us, just as the universe itself embodies goodness, and through that goodness we come to realize ourselves, our relation with our families, our society, our world, and the universe itself. As Okada would say, we simply need to realize the basic premise of Confucius' teaching, his teaching of goodness, which is found in the text known as the *Analects*, the record of the sayings of Confucius. This teaching has played a central role in the life and cultures of East and Southeast Asia for the past twenty-five hundred years.

Confucius: The Man and the Message

Who is this man Confucius, and what is this work called the *Analects*, that twenty-five hundred years later people are still discussing his ideas, attempting to emulate his teachings, and suggesting that those teachings are as relevant today as they were in his own time? What can we derive from reading these words of an ancient Chinese thinker in our own lives and our own time? Can these teachings change the way we look at ourselves, at our world, at the aspirations and goals of our lives? Can these teachings bring peace and understanding to each person and to the world, as Confucius himself hoped? Can we find an answer to who we are and the nature of the quest that occupies each of our lives?

Confucius speaks in remarkably simple words and a gentle tone, yet the meaning of his teachings can occupy a lifetime of learning. As his own disciples said of him, his depth and his wisdom know no bounds. Trying to penetrate them, you find that they are only deeper and always beyond full grasp (*Analects* IX:10). However many steps are taken, his own depth of understanding lies always ahead (*Analects* XIX:23). Throughout East and Southeast Asia his words have provided a foundation for defining our ultimate nature—the moral nature that is central to our being and to the universe itself. His message moves the individual toward that realization of goodness, what we can refer to as the path of the sage.

Confucius' Life of Learning

Confucius (551–479 BCE) was born in the state of Lu, a small state now part of Shantung province. His personal name was K'ung Ch'iu, a son in the K'ung family. The family appears to have descended from a noble family but was impoverished by the time of Confucius' birth. His father is said to have died when Confucius was very young and his mother died when he was sixteen. Virtually nothing is known about his childhood, though he apparently married when he was eighteen. His own autobiographical statement in the *Analects* asserts that he began his learning at fifteen (*Analects* II:4), though we have no details about either the context or the content of this learning. What we do know is that his reputation for learning and teaching appears to have grown rapidly and with it he eventually came to be called K'ung Tzu, Master K'ung, or K'ung Fu Tzu, Great Master K'ung, the latter Latinized by the Jesuits centuries later into the name we all recognize, "Confucius."

Confucius is considered to have been a member of a class of people known as *ju*, which became the standard term for Confucianism with its rise to prominence following Confucius' death. The term itself actually means "weakling" and refers to the class of people who were scholars; that is, they were "weak" because they did not work with their bodies, but with their minds! Confucius himself is portrayed in the *Analects* as someone who simply loves learning, the learning of the ancient sages, *sheng*, and desires to teach their learning in the hope that it can provide a path for people, society, and the world at large to come to the ways of goodness. To fulfill the teachings of the sages, for Confucius, was to transform the world into a state of goodness. Confucius' role was a simple one—he was a scholar and a teacher who believed that the works he studied, the works called the Classics, *ching*, passed down from early times and representing the ancient ways, provided a way of learning that could bring peace and understanding to individuals and society alike.

Confucius lived in a time of increasing social, political, and religious chaos, the beginning of the disintegration of the Chou Dynasty (1045–256 BCE) into a series of contending and competing separate states, a period in Chinese history called the Spring and Autumn (722–479 BCE). During Confucius' adult life records indicate he held a series of minor government positions. He eventually rose as high as prime minister of the state of Lu before abandoning all official titles because of his disaffection for what he saw as the corruption of court life. Following his court experience he traveled from state to state with a group of his disciples, attempting to convince the rulers of the states to return to the ways of the sages of antiquity and thus rebuild the moral virtue he saw as the governing principle of the early Chou Dynasty. After some fourteen years and little success in the venture, he returned to his native state of Lu.

Aging in years, he gathered a greater number of disciples as he turned exclusively to teaching the ways of the ancient sages. Confucius believed that the world could be restored to a time of peace and harmony if all people, rulers and commoners alike, would set aside their ways of selfishness and aggression and return to the teachings of goodness, the moral capacity of humankind that ultimately reflects the moral structure of the universe and is exemplified by the words and deeds of the sages recorded in the Classics. He believed it possible to invoke this change in both self and society because he had the record of the time of the sages when the world was at peace in the distant past.

Not unlike other religious figures, Confucius strongly believed that there was a model of true goodness that had existed in the past, what we might call a golden age. Many have looked to such a time, and humankind has often built its hopes upon the capacity of a particular person or set of ideas and practices to successfully navigate a return to a time of greater purity and innocence. In a sense it is the quest for utopia and may be as basic to human nature as the quest for life itself. Every generation, it seems, looks to an earlier time, a beginning time, if only to reactivate the possibility of human potential and the goal of human transformation against the sheer weight of human inertia.

Before his own death in 479 BCE, Confucius witnessed the death of his wife, his son, and his closest disciple, Yen Yüan. At his own death, though he had little official recognition, he had what appears to have been a significant number of disciples committed to carrying on his teachings. He summarized his own life in his short autobiographical account (*Analects* II:4), describing himself as a man devoted to learning and fully embodying the teachings of the ancient sages.

The *Analects*: Unique Wisdom

The *Analects* of Confucius, called *Lun Yü* in Chinese, is regarded as the most accurate and complete account of the life and teachings of Confucius. It was compiled after his death by his disciples from their notes of comments Confucius made or records of some of the short dialogues he engaged in with rulers of his day. Very little is known about the actual textual history of the work. The first references to the *Analects* are found in a Han Dynasty (ca. 200 BCE–220 CE) Confucian work of the first centuries before the Common Era. There were generally considered to have been three versions of the text, with only one of those surviving to contemporary times. The surviving version seems to have originated in Confucius' native area of the state of Lu. It was divided into two parts, each with ten books, or *chüan*, the designation for the structural division of the text. Most often scholars suggest that there is no major structure or organizing principle to the passages; however, there is some internal grouping of topics, though it appears rudimentary at best.

After its compilation, the *Analects* rose as a central work to the emerging Confucian tradition and it became the tradition's foundational text, a position it has held to the present day. Grouped with the Classics, its primary utilization was study and learning. Thus it was studied and memorized as the Classics were, and as Confucianism emerged as the dominant state ideology, it assumed a role as a critical source of official education. Its use, of course, was largely confined to the educated class. Given the low level of literacy and limited number of copies of any text, which were the product of hand copying, the actual "readership" must have been very small. However, those who did read and study the work played important roles in the evolving leadership and administration of the Chinese state.

When compared with scripture of other religious traditions, the *Analects* differs markedly from equivalent foundational texts, a point often used to suggest the difference between Confucianism and other religious traditions. The *Analects* is not a work purported to be directly revealed to humankind from some higher source, like the Hebrew Bible, Qur'an, or Vedas. It does not place its founder and principal teacher, Confucius, in an elevated status or ascribe to him supernatural features, and it does not suggest its own unique role and mission as a revelation of truth, as do, for example, the Christian Scriptures with the uniqueness of Jesus. The name *Analects*, the traditional translation of its Chinese title, means simply "conversations" or "dialogues." It is nothing more than the recorded sayings and short dialogues between Confucius and his disciples and some of the rulers of the day. But with this record of simple statements in the *Analects*, the tradition is established and its growth and development are a matter of history.

The Emergence of the Confucian Tradition

Based upon what we know of his life and his own attempts to influence political conditions of his day, Confucius might be regarded as remarkably *unsuccessful* in turning around the fortunes of the Chou Dynasty or creating a new state of true moral virtue. He was, after all, unable to convince a single ruler to accept his advice and teaching to transform the world from a condition of chaos to the rule of the sages of antiquity. Still, he attracted wide attention and gathered a large number of disciples who continued to argue for his quest of returning the world to a state of harmony.

In the decades and centuries following the death of Confucius, the condition of the world that was the center of Confucius' pleas only worsened. China moved into an era called the Warring States Period (479–221 BCE) simply because of the level of internecine warfare taking place among contending states, all of which were attempting to replace the steadily weakening Chou Dynasty. What began as a large number of such warring states gradually reduced itself to a smaller number of more and more powerful states. Near the end of this period, there were only three states contending for power—Ch'in, Ch'u, and Ch'i—in an environment of ever increasing civil strife.

Ironically, the Warring States Period represented a remarkable time in the development of all the major systems of traditional Chinese thought and thus was also called the Period of the Hundred Schools of Thought. This produced not only Confucius and Classical Confucianism but also Early Taoism represented by Lao-tzu and Chuang-tzu. In addition, the Yin/Yang School, the Legalist School, the Agriculturalist School, the Mohist School, and a variety of other perspectives developed. Not unlike the Greek and Indian worlds of the same time, Chinese thought in the several centuries before the beginning of the Common Era showed remarkable development, creativity, and transformation in the areas of philosophy and religion. This common occurrence across three major and completely diverse areas of the ancient world occasioned the German philosopher Karl Jaspers to refer to this phenomenon as a worldwide Axial Age of philosophy and religion,[1] an interesting idea to reflect upon.

The Warring States Period ended with the victory of the Ch'in state and with it the establishment of the Ch'in Dynasty (221–207 BCE). Following the short-lived Ch'in Dynasty came the Han Dynasty, a long and stable period that saw the development of major and lasting trends in Chinese religion and philosophy. An indication of these major trends was the onset of references to China as the land of Three Religions, *san chiao*, that is, Taoism, Buddhism, and Confucianism. During this period, Taoism transformed itself from the early and very individualistic Taoist philosophy found in the *Tao Te Ching* and the *Chuang-tzu* to the religion of Taoism of later generations, the high liturgical religion still represented in China today. Buddhism entered China from India and began to integrate into Chinese culture, changing in its representation and forming unique Chinese Buddhist teachings such as Ch'an Buddhism and its more popular Japanese form, Zen Buddhism. And finally, Confucianism was established as the official ideology of the Chinese state. In this role it can be described as the state religion of China, a religion made up largely of the ruling elite and their bureaucracy, a position it also occupied throughout East and Southeast Asian cultures until the twentieth century.

That Confucianism became official state ideology shows a very large change in its role and status within the culture generally. From its position as one school among the Hundred Schools of Thought, it became the dominant school of thought. What happened to make this change possible after the seeming failure of its founder to solicit even the faintest interest of a single ruler of his day? The tradition of study did not stop, and thus Confucius' focus on the Classics as the key to learning became recognized and their promulgation further encouraged. The first university opened in 124 BCE to offer a curriculum in the study of the Classics. The Chinese civil service examination system also began around that time and focused on the training of those who would assume leadership positions in service to the state. Then as well as throughout history, and very much unlike the training in the West, the curriculum was an education in the Classics—an education in humanistic learning rather than technical knowledge.

The rest is history, literally and figuratively. Confucianism continued to hold a position of state orthodoxy throughout almost all of Chinese history. The tradition also grew in intellectual and philosophical sophistication, becoming a dominant intellectual tradition generally called Neo-Confucianism beginning in the eleventh century and continuing until the present day. With the expansion of the Chinese sphere of influence throughout East and Southeast Asia, Chinese thought spread to the cultures of Korea, Japan, and Southeast Asia. In this broadening sphere of influence, Confucianism played a remarkably significant role in these diverse cultures, assuming a position of leadership within the structure of the state as well as philosophical leadership across varying ideologies. This position was retained until the pressure of modernity in the twentieth century radically transformed East and Southeast Asian cultures with the forces of revolution and Western ideologies. Yet even with the common appraisal that Confucianism is now moribund in its official role as state ideology, there is still a broad adaptation of Confucian values thoroughly diffused throughout these cultures today, and, as we will see, Confucianism is as much a teaching for the self as it is for society.

Teachings of the *Analects*

As we have seen, Confucius was simply a student and teacher with a love of learning. His focus was the wisdom of the ancient sages as embodied in the Classics. His teachings were his transmission and interpretation of the words and deeds of the sages. The sages of Confucius' particular attention were Yao and Shun, ancient sage kings who purportedly lived during the second millennium BCE, and Kings Wen and Wu and the Duke of Chou, the founding figures of the Chou Dynasty in the eleventh century BCE. Confucius found in the descriptions of their attitudes and actions and their purported words and deeds the model to return the world to peace and order and the individual to moral goodness. It was in Confucius' mind a "golden age," and is referenced in Chinese as the *ta-tung*, the period of Great Unity.

There is, however, much more to the story of the rise of Confucianism to a position of prominence than simply its teaching of governance of the state, as important as that role was historically. A major reason for the spread of Confucian values, in fact, has little to do with state ideology. Confucianism was from the very beginning a system of personal learning and self-cultivation, what Confucius referred to as "learning for the self," *wei chi* (*Analects* XIV:25). Confucian goals for the state were peace and harmony for society, but the Confucian goal for the individual was the attempt to emulate the ways of the ancient sages within his or her life. Self and society are not separate; Confucian teachings to bring morality to the state were also an exercise in manifesting goodness within the individual, the fundamental connection between self-understanding and moral action on behalf of others.

At the very center of these teachings of moral cultivation in Confucianism was the concept of *jen*, goodness, a term that defined the proper relation of one person to another. Translations such as "goodness" or "humaneness" build from this fundamental sense of the proper relation between persons. When asked to define *jen*, Tseng-tzu, one of Confucius' disciples, described it as the single thread, *i-i-kuan-chih*, that runs through the Master's teaching. Clarifying the term further, he called it *chung*, loyalty, and *shu*, reciprocity or empathy. In Confucius' own words, "Do not do to others what you would not want them to do to you" (*Analects* XII:2, XV:23). In the first known written formulation of the "Golden Rule" Confucius emphasized that people should act with kindness, empathy, and love. Confucius made this teaching the quintessential expression of his understanding of human goodness, *jen*, and the single thread that is his most central teaching.

This same emphasis upon goodness, *jen*, is seen in another central Confucian teaching, filial piety, *hsiao*, the relation of parents and children grounded in love and acted upon through care and nurturing for the young and old alike. Filial piety was seen as a reciprocal relation for Confucius. As parents take care of children when they are young, so children take care of parents when they age. In Confucianism, such relations and thus such virtues are considered *natural*, that is, what should be the case, because of the naturalness of moral relations, and in the case of filial piety, special moral relations. The world Confucius lived in, however, was anything but moral and thus he attempted to challenge the ways of his day with a plea to return to a time where he believed filial relations were grounded in true goodness, a basic moral code. Such morality, Confucius believed, is simply part of our nature.

What such teachings mean for the individual, for the learning of the self, is a commitment to moral development of the individual. The earnestness and complete devotion of this commitment is often overlooked in favor of a particular virtue, such as filial piety, but it lies at the very heart of Confucius' teachings. People live with and through moral virtue. Such moral virtue is based on acting with rightness or righteousness, *i*, and truthfulness or faithfulness, *hsin*, terms that delve deep into the interior capacity of the self to reflect upon itself in moral terms and thus act in moral ways. On the basis of the inward moral rectitude reflected by *i* and *hsin*, a person understands the capacity for outward moral commitment and action. The movement is from interior reflection to outward action.

With moral rectitude of the self as the focus, we move to another central concept of Confucius' teaching, his sense of the importance of *li*, translated as "rites" or "propriety." The relationship between moral learning and ritual is captured in a phrase in the *Analects* that translates as "disciplining the self and returning to the rites" (*Analects* XII:1). Confucius lived in a world of ritual performance. Rituals were performed to mark major life events, including birth, death, and marriage; to honor ancestors (ancestor worship); and at state ceremonies. Sacrifice and libations were a model for the order and structure of the world. What Confucius witnessed, however, was a world beginning to disintegrate, as evidenced by the Warring States Period. In that world of increasing chaos, with power no longer found in the rulers of the Chou Dynasty, rulers attempted to maintain a semblance of power through the performance of ritual. Thus, in a world of diminishing political power, rituals were maintained and perhaps even overemphasized. Given the rulers' vain display of such authority, Confucius focused not upon the ritual *performance*, but instead upon the significance of a person's *attitude* in ritual, suggesting that ritual was something deeper than just the performance itself. He often commented about ritual performance by rulers of his day, suggesting that their rituals should be more than simply correct deportment and properly measured liturgy. What he felt was missing was feeling, an inner sense of the solemnity of ritual, and the expression of propriety in the ritual act.

But what was the propriety expressed toward? Remember the context—the teaching of the sages of antiquity—all of it suggesting seriousness or reverence, *ching*, a critically important attitude for Confucius. What Confucius deemed essential was seriousness and reverence directed toward what he believed the sages saw as the final source of authority, *T'ien*, translated as Heaven, the high God of the Chou Dynasty. As he surveyed the landscape of his day and the dwindling authority of the Chou state and the rising hegemonic rule of contending states, Confucius saw no exercise of propriety. Yes, there was ritual performance, but it lacked the critical component, the reverence shown the final source of authority, Heaven itself. Confucius believed neither self nor society could achieve goodness with this lack of reverence toward Heaven. The status of that final source of authority upon which all Confucian teachings are based poses the question of the degree to which Confucius is, in fact, a thoroughly religious figure and thus the founder of a tradition that, while often mistaken as merely a form of humanistic ethics, is deeply religious and spiritual. As such, Confucius taught the path of the sage, the treading of what he called the Way of Heaven, *T'ien Tao* (*Analects* V:12).

The Path of the Sage

The teachings we have discussed represent a wide variety of what we might describe as individual virtues. For Confucius, the virtues are embodied or realized in an ideal figure, someone who has developed and fully realized such traits. That ideal figure, surprisingly, is *not* the sage. Confucius saw the sages, *sheng*, as very distant figures far from an ideal that might be realized for him or his disciples. For Confucius, the sages were only figures of high antiquity who, as paragons of virtue and emulates of Heaven's Way, stood as the models for which humankind could be judged but for whom the ideal remained distant. Instead, Confucius focused on a figure referred to as the *chün tzu*, best translated as Noble Person or Profound Person. Originally, it was a term that described a person born into the aristocracy; however, Confucius changed the meaning to suggest that the title was no longer a mark of birth but a designation of moral cultivation and the embodiment of goodness. Frequently in the *Analects* Confucius contrasts the Noble Person with the petty person, *hsiao jen*, and finds only the example of the Noble Person worthy of emulation. For example, the Noble Person places demands upon himself; the petty person blames others (*Analects* XV:20). The Noble Person concentrates upon what is right; the petty person only thinks of what is profitable (*Analects* IV:16). Bottom line, the Noble Person takes responsibility for his actions and makes whatever sacrifices are necessary to fulfill the ideal of goodness.

For Confucius, to become a Noble Person is to emulate the path of the sage. It is to realize that every person has the capacity to embody the Way of Heaven. It is to live a life in accord with self and society and thus in harmony with the words and deeds of the sages of antiquity and the Way of Heaven. The goal is fulfilled through a life of learning, where all life's actions become occasions for reflection and for the understanding of the self. There is no action and no thought that is not part of the learning process. All learning sets the foundation for goodness. Such a life manifests itself through empathy and reciprocity for the trials and tribulations of all other persons. The teaching is to realize goodness in the self and goodness in society at large and manifest it in all thoughts and actions. As one who embodies the Golden Rule, the Noble Person is thus a Profound Person.

And this, the Profound Person, is the religious character of the Confucian goal. It is not focused upon a transformation toward some condition after the termination of life, not some higher state, not some "other" reality, not "salvation" as might be defined by Western Abrahamic traditions or "liberation" as sought by Hinduism or "enlightenment" as centered by the Buddhist tradition. There is no place you go, no place you leave, no renunciation of life, no cycle of birth and rebirth. In theological terms, there is no eschatology pointing to a state beyond life. Rather, the Confucian reaches fulfillment within the context of life itself, this life. In Confucian thought, the universe spins its way through countless changes and transformations. It is not capricious or random; there is order and harmony in the constant transformations of all things, and humankind is a part of that order and harmony. There is no need for a separate and continuous existence, for an eternity of individuality or an eternity of unity; there is only the recognition that you are part of the process. This is the Way of Heaven pointed to by the path of the sage and fulfilled in love and goodness. Confucius said that he would take his final rest in *jen* (*Analects* IV:2), the goodness inherent in all things, and upon hearing the Way in the morning, he could die content in the evening (*Analects* IV:8).

Ultimate meaning, ultimate self-understanding is found within this life itself. You can ask for nothing more, and you are at peace. Such teachings bring a level of understanding that suggest a moral capacity and thus a spiritual depth transcending any historical or cultural boundaries. The depth and lasting qualities of this tradition make it a viable teaching and equally relevant for the individual from Confucius' day to our own.

Gender in Confucian Tradition

Confucianism was a completely male-dominated tradition. It focused on the sages of antiquity, all male, and sought to establish moral rulers, also all male. It generally sought to severely limit the role of women to "traditional" roles. The Noble Person was understood as essentially only male in the time of Confucius, and this understanding is reflected in the *Analects* and the translation here.

Later, however, women began to be included in the tradition. In fact, a text called *Analects for Women*, *Nü Lun Yü*, sought to emphasize the ability of women to learn and perfect Confucian teachings within the roles assigned to women. In the much later context of Neo-Confucian thought, but mainly in more radical schools, it was recognized that women, too, had the capacity for sagehood.

Although the text historically was male-centered, the implications of this teaching are gender-neutral and can be appreciated by anyone.

The Classics and the *Analects*: The Nature of the Works

At the center of Confucianism and foundational to its message and development stand the Classics and the *Analects*. They were grouped together and canonized as an enshrinement of the learning Confucius advocated throughout his life.

In the earliest grouping there are generally considered to be Five Classics, the Classics of Change, Poetry, History, Ritual, and the Spring and Autumn, though more works were added in later times. These are literary works that originated across many centuries and purport to represent the earliest times of Chinese history and civilization. They were probably created in their earliest forms during the first centuries of the Chou Dynasty, though they were still in development even after Confucius' lifetime. Because of this time span, one of the questions often raised is just how much of the Classics as we have them today were seen and studied by Confucius. There has also been a strong tradition that even associated Confucius with, if not the composition of parts of the Classics, at least editorial work on them.

The first of the five principal Classics, the *I Ching*, or *Book of Changes*, was originally a book of divination; its initial layers were very early Chou period and essentially took the structure of divinatory formulas. Over time, more materials were added to the work, commentary layers called the Ten Wings, and the resulting work became a major source of philosophical and religious discussion throughout Chinese history as well as throughout East and Southeast Asia.

Second, the *Shih Ching*, or *Book of Poetry*, is a collection of some three hundred poems that represent a wide range of topics and are often interpreted to be folk songs in origin. Confucius was thought to have edited the work into its final form. Although Confucians interpret this work as the expression of moral virtue, others have seen the work as simply masterpieces of poetic form having no particular moral message.

Third, the *Shu Ching*, or *Book of History*, purports to represent a record of the most ancient history of China from the very beginning, including periods still not substantiated by historical research. Its most important feature, however, is its focus upon the sages of high antiquity, Yao and Shun, said to have lived long before even the first dynasty, and the founders of the Chou Dynasty, Kings Wen and Wu and the Duke of Chou. It includes materials telling of their deeds and even purported speeches. This material became the basis for much of Confucius' view of the ways of virtue of the ancients.

Fourth, what we refer to as the Classic of Ritual, generally called *Li Chi*, *Record of Ritual*, includes great detail about ritual from the early Chou Dynasty as well as more philosophical interpretations of the meaning of ritual. This collection of works, in whatever forms Confucius saw them, played a large role in his belief in the centrality of ritual and its potential for a deep and profound aspect of human consciousness.

Lastly, the *Ch'un Ch'iu*, *Spring and Autumn Annals*, is a detailed history of the state of Lu. Although it was only a small and insignificant state, Lu was the birthplace of Confucius. The fact that its history warrants the status of a Classic suggests the degree to which Confucius gained extraordinary stature as the generations passed.

While not all individually titled *ching*, what we render as "classic" in English, they are collectively titled the Classics and will be so titled even as the number of works that make up the collection increases over time. The origin of the term *ching* comes from the handicraft of weaving and means the warp threads, the threads that run lengthwise in a piece of cloth. A warp provides the continuity and foundation of a piece of cloth, and by implication a Classic is a work that underlies a culture, that cuts across time to apply to any generation. The same term, however, when applied to Buddhist or Taoist writings, is translated as "scripture." Why the difference? Inherent in the translation is the perspective that the Confucian tradition is not religious and thus it can have Classics, but not scripture.

The Classics are said to be the recorded words and deeds of the sages of antiquity. When we analyze the Chinese character for sage, *sheng*, we find that it is composed of two parts. One part suggests a person who has heard something. The earliest Chinese dictionary, the *Shuo Wen*, tells us that what the sage hears is the Way of *T'ien*, Heaven, the high God of the Chou Dynasty, and what will become the Absolute and Infinite Principle, the Transcendent, for the Confucian tradition throughout its history. The second part of the character means "he who manifests" or "puts into action." Thus the term for sage means, "he who hears the Way of Heaven and manifests it for humankind." With this as the core meaning for the sage and the origin of the Classics said to be the sages, it follows that the Classics most certainly have a sacred source for their origins and thus are appropriately called scripture, Confucian scripture.

The *Analects* are not regarded as a Classic, but they are grouped with the Classics when canonized. However, it is important to remember Confucius' own description of his role and mission as recorded in the *Analects*. He said that he was not a creator, but only a transmitter (*Analects* VII:1). While other religious founders might well regard themselves as transmitters, they see themselves as transmitters of a transcendent order—a God and God's commands, for example. Such a transmitter is essentially a human vessel for this communication from on high. Is Confucius different in his self-appraisal from this more typical illustration of a religious founder even when the origin of the Classics is the sages hearing the Way of Heaven?

The answer is yes, because Confucius saw himself as self-consciously only responsible for transmitting what had already been created in the historic past and recorded in historical materials from that time. He was a transmitter of the ways of the ancient sages as contained in the Classics. He viewed himself as transmitting what could primarily be called history, not a revelation of a transcendent order or an epiphany of transcendent truth. His sayings and dialogues as recorded in the *Analects* have become the interpretative tool of the Classics and the teachings represented in them.

Given this interpretation, are the Classics still sacred works? This is a question that is rather more complex. They are certainly not like the Hebrew Bible or the Christian Scriptures in terms of the revelation of the commandments of God to Moses or the presentation of the uniqueness of a single and religiously transformative figure such as Jesus and his role in salvation history. However, the Classics do represent the ways of the sages and connect the human sphere to the sphere of Heaven, *T'ien,* what we could interpret as the Confucian source of the Transcendent. As such, they are religious and thus can be said to bear the authority conveyed by the term "scripture," though they still seem to differ from other examples of scripture that we might more readily identify. It is a complex question because we do not want to lose the sense of a Confucian scripture on the one hand, but we also need to distinguish Confucian scripture from other models of scripture where the emphasis rests with the obvious appearance of a transcendent source, a sense of revelation and epiphany.

And what of the *Analects*? Are we to extend the category of scripture to the *Analects*? To adequately account for the role it plays in the history of the Confucian tradition and to express its own role in the establishment of the Classics as Confucian scripture, we can only suggest that the profound religious meaning of Confucius' teachings and the *Analects* as the embodiment of those teachings render the *Analects* as a profound religious work in itself. Yes, the *Analects* are Confucian scripture. Any conclusion as to the religious status of the Confucian canon, however, is meaningful only to the degree to which the founder of the tradition may himself be regarded as religious.

Confucius—Religious Teacher?

No question has been raised more in the study of the Confucian tradition and of Confucius himself than whether Confucius and his teachings may be regarded as religious. Most scholarship has concluded that there is little about the tradition, and perhaps even less about the teachings of its founder, that could be called religious. A very long tradition of scholarship has suggested that Confucius, instead of being a formulator of a religious tradition, is rather more the founder of a form of humanism where ethics play a central role, but where there is nothing to suggest that the teachings lead toward a religious goal.

The work of Wing-tsit Chan and Fung Yu-lan, both major Confucian philosophers of the twentieth century, build their interpretation of Confucius and the Confucian tradition upon the basis of its humanist roots and its revolutionary role as a form of *humanism* in the face of traditional Chinese religion and superstition. This view, when placed in the context of a modernizing China, was a basis of arguing for a Confucian tradition that had the capacity to transform China into its modern state rather than hold it in a quagmire of traditional ways. Majority interpretation has suggested until quite recently, however, that Confucianism was precisely what held China back from fully adopting modernization. Only in the past twenty years has there been a major shift in interpretation that now sees Confucianism with its focus on learning as posing a kind of intellectual openness that was critical to modernization, rather than a bastion of resistance. However, even in its positive role, Confucianism will be largely interpreted as a form of humanism devoid of religious sentiment.

To bolster the claim of humanism in the *Analects* there are several passages frequently cited that purport to demonstrate not so much a religious as an agnostic stance. One passage suggests that you are to keep spirits and ghosts at a distance (*Analects* VI:20). Another suggests that you conduct sacrifice *as if* the spirits were there (*Analects* III:12). Still another passage suggests that the Master does not talk of supernatural things (*Analects* VII:20). And finally, there is a passage that suggests that when the Master was asked about death he responded by saying that he did not know about life and therefore certainly could not know about death (*Analects* XI:11). Are these passages the deathblow to a religious interpretation of Confucius and the *Analects*?

The question, of course, is whether any of these passages actually discredit a religious perspective, especially when measured against passages that demonstrate a deep and profound sense of a religious perspective. Consider, for example, our earlier reference to Confucius' autobiographical passage (*Analects* II:4). In autobiographical form Confucius described a life committed to learning, and thus potentially humanism, but he went on to suggest that such learning was focused on realizing and following the Way of Heaven, something he said he accomplished by the age of seventy. In other passages his descriptions of the Noble Person

suggest someone coming to realize his own goodness and finding ultimate meaning in that realization. We may have to redefine certain features of the Confucian religious perspective, but there is little doubt that
for Confucius learning and teaching are focused on studying the way of
the sages, who in turn reflect the Way of Heaven, *T'ien Tao*, a source of
ultimate meaning and thus peace.

Although the humanistic quality of Confucius' thinking is obvious,
whether we dismiss religion or spirituality from his thought arises in part
from the problem inherent in our own use of the term "humanism." In
our times we often think of humanism as opposed to religion, thus the
popular use of the term "secular humanism," particularly in the culture
wars of our day. The reason this equation is made is because humanism
for us is defined largely by the European Enlightenment of the seven-
teenth century, the intellectual revolution that promoted the dominance
of empiricism to the exclusion of religious thinking. What is so easily
forgotten in this model is the humanism that emerged from the earlier
European Renaissance of the thirteenth century, where humanism was
fully informed by religious sentiment. If we take the earlier definition,
that is, Renaissance religious humanism, then we can better appreciate
the potential of Confucianism to reflect both the growing influence of
humanism and its inherent religious or spiritual foundation. In this spirit
we can appreciate the humanism of Confucius as a source of religious
and spiritual value.

Relevance of the *Analects*

The *Analects* might be said to be "long ago and far away," and we can
ask ourselves why read it, why study it, why be concerned with its teachings? I am sure I wondered at my own first reading of the *Analects* why I
should care about the teachings of Confucius and what possible relevance they have for the modern world and contemporary society. But
that was a long time ago for me. The years have passed, but this is a text
I continue to come back to, not just because I teach it in the curriculum of

a university, but also because the text has a peculiar way of making itself relevant in setting after setting.

The *Analects* probes and pushes toward questioning and understanding. It holds up the individual for self-examination. It holds up the world we have created for critique. The work is strong in its recommendations and uncompromising in its moral and religious message, and yet the tone is gentle, subtle, and quiet in its reflective capacity.

I have come to the conclusion that at one level it *is* a classic, just as the Chinese determined, because it appeals across time to any generation and, as we have seen, it also appeals across cultural boundaries. Its capacity to engage in this pan-historic and cross-cultural context reflects a higher level of understanding and significance, its ability to raise the universal questions of humankind and to provide answers in ways that suggest a path for humanity to follow toward their own self-understanding and the betterment of themselves and the world.

The *Analects* has been studied and ruminated upon throughout its history. In more contemporary times it has been the subject of extensive scholarship as well as multiple translations. What I have tried to do in this volume differs substantially from contemporary work with the text. This is not a scholarly work per se, but at the same time it does not disregard the traditions of scholarship. My style, rather than Western academic scholarship, resembles far more the tradition of Chinese historical commentary, where such commentary addressed the meaning of the text in terms of the meaning of the teachings for the individual and thus the relevance of the teachings to the life of each reader.

As I struggle with the issue of meaning, I want to share my own inclinations as to the understanding of these teachings with you. I don't pretend to have conclusions about meaning and understanding, only possible avenues of approach. But these avenues toward meaning and understanding will, I hope, provide you with a set of questions and perhaps some answers that will bring further reflection upon yourself and society and the world we live in.

It turns out that sixth-century BCE China and our own world are not after all so very distant or distinct. The sad note is that humankind today finds itself in pretty much the same position as those who lived in the declining years of the Chou Dynasty. Uncontrolled and incessant warfare, untold human suffering and misery, unspeakable contrast of wealth and poverty, unconscionable self-interest over service to others, failure to live by the Golden Rule—all are characteristics of then and now. Even more troublesome is the observation that there has been little reprieve across historical or cultural boundaries and few alternatives to these conditions, ever!

So to the question, "Is the *Analects* relevant today?" the answer is a resounding "yes," expressed with the hope that humanity can finally address its capacity to live with goodness and see goodness in others, in a willingness to finally live by the single thread that runs through all these teachings, the Golden Rule.

When asked about the future of Confucianism, Okada Takehiko responded by saying that the name of a particular religion or Way was entirely unimportant. The only thing that was important was for each individual to develop his capacity for goodness and to live his life as an embodiment of this goodness. The issue is not calling goodness by its Confucian name or Christian name or Buddhist name or any other name for that matter. The importance lies only in living our lives through goodness in the community of all humanity and all things in the universe—that is our goal, that is our fulfillment, that is the path of the sage.

Coda: A Word about Translation
Selecting passages from a work as rich in nuanced textures as the *Analects* is a challenge of the first order. I have, however, tried to select those passages that seem most central to uncovering what I consider the philosophical, religious, and spiritual dimensions of the work. Still, there are many passages not included and some only referenced, but I hope these selections will spur you on to further reading and self-discovery in the work as a whole.

To date there have been numerous translations of the *Analects* in languages too numerous to reiterate. Suffice it to say that there are translations in most major languages of the world and a few minor ones as well. This also includes translations in modern Chinese, because the language of the original text is *wen yen*, or Classical Chinese. The text is essentially twenty-five hundred years old and the style of language is a written language only, not a spoken one, and fundamentally different from modern Chinese in terms of both grammar and vocabulary.

For the translation I have followed several conventions. First, because of the ease of reading Chinese terms when rendered in our alphabet, I have chosen the older Wade-Giles system of Romanization. While the newer Pinyin system has been utilized widely, I don't believe that it facilitates the reader's ability to pronounce Chinese words as easily as the older Wade-Giles system. Second, I am of course familiar with many of the translations that are available and admire a number of them for their accuracy of translation and at times the beauty of the language. In this context, translations that should be mentioned as possible sources for consultation and variations include Arthur Waley, the dean of Western translations of Chinese literature; D. C. Lau, who has provided us with some of the most approachable and accurate renderings of multiple Chinese thinkers; and Wing-tsit Chan, who represents a distinctly Confucian translation. My own preference, however, has been to return to the nineteenth-century translation by the noted Sinologist James Legge (1815–1897).

I have selected Legge's translation for several reasons. For many years I have been extraordinarily impressed with Legge's rendering of the grammar of the text, something I am not sure always remains intact in some translations. There are, however, more subtle reasons. These have to do with the ability to communicate a twenty-five-hundred-year-old text with a sense of its solemnity of age and its seriousness of intent. For as simple a text as the content of the *Analects* represents, it has been treated with seriousness and reverence across its history that justifies careful grammatical structure and selected word choice. Although the goal is to communicate the content of the text, frankly, a little eloquence in translation communicates not only the position the work has been held in but also the seriousness and reverence held by the disciples of Confucius who recorded the work.

James Legge was a fascinating man. It took many years for him to admit to the depth of Confucius' teachings. His early church background set the parameters for his appreciation of other forms of religious expression. Near the end of his life, however, in his final edition of his translation of the *Analects*, he suggested that he had come to see the wisdom, depth, and profundity of Confucius. As such, his translation can be seen as embedded with an appreciation of the ways in which Confucius and the *Analects* can be understood as a source of spiritual and religious insight. The religious character of James Legge is a fascinating issue and one that has been explored at length in the wonderful scholarship of Norman Girardot in the reconstruction of Legge's life.[2] My own perspective is that Legge, through his own deep and profound Christian commitment, eventually came to see the capacity for depth in Confucius, as radical a suggestion as that might have been in the Victorian world in which he lived!

I have made changes from Legge's rendering in terms of more contemporary word choice for certain basic Confucian teachings and a change now and then of any stilted structure that may too quickly suggest Victorian usage. Readability and communication are, after all, paramount but so, too, are eloquence and the reverential tone and attitude embedded in Confucius' sayings and dialogues.

Finally, the occasional italicized words in the translated passages are Legge's insertions where he felt that an additional word or phrase was needed to fill out the meaning of what often was a very abbreviated statement in the text itself. These add to the richness of the textual rendering. I believe that Legge presents us with a unique opportunity to have an accurate rendering of the text, one that draws upon the richness of the English language to express the text's subtleties as well as the reverence in which the text should be held. My respect for the preservation of Legge's renderings is very high, as is the honor in which I hold him for his contribution to our understanding of Confucius and the *Analects*.

1 □ Opening the *Analects*: The Pursuit of Learning

Most major Chinese religious and philosophical writings begin with a passage that introduces you to the work as a whole. Historically, a good deal of the learning process involved memorization, and there was no better way to begin your recitation of a work than with a passage or statement that set out the agenda for the work as a whole. Probably the most famous example of this convention is found in the opening passage of the well-known Taoist classic, the *Tao Te Ching*. In a few characters the quintessential teaching of the work as a whole is laid out and commented upon with a succinctness at which you cannot but marvel: "The Way that can be spoken of is not the eternal Way; the Name that can be named is not the eternal Name."

In the *Analects*, it is almost as if the first passage were specifically designated for the role it would play across twenty-five hundred years of Confucian history. In this very brief passage are to be found the most basic and cardinal principles that define the very nature of Confucianism. What should be noted from the outset is the rather ordinary nature of the content of the passage. Ironically, the very commonness of its style and content becomes the trademark of its depth.

1 Learning, *hsüeh*, is a word of extraordinary importance to the Confucian tradition; it is the beginning of all Confucian teaching. It defines a path for humankind to follow to reach self-understanding, peace in the world, and rapport with the Way of Heaven, *T'ien Tao*, the absolute purpose within all things. For Confucius, such learning comes from the sages of antiquity and is contained in the works called the Classics or Confucian scripture. This wisdom is always accessible to humankind through learning, not as some mysterious and esoteric process. The human mind is considered rational and capable of ultimate understanding.

2 This is not a teaching that demands isolation and retreat from the world but rather welcomes the opportunity of learning in the company of others. It also suggests that such learning is not limited just to reading and study of the Classics, but can be found in any encounter within life. Life itself is the great teacher of the Way of Heaven, and here Confucius suggests the importance of human friendship as a basis for continual learning. We find in friendship a foundation for the moral character that is our nature and a reflection of the Way of Heaven.

3 The Noble Person, *chün tzu*, is focused on learning that patterns itself on the sages of antiquity and the Way of Heaven. While you might hope that a person of moral worth would find his way to a position of leadership in the world, the Noble Person does not sour should such learning remain unrecognized. In simple and ordinary language and thought, the *Analects* begins on a note of utter humility.

The Master said, "Is it not a joy to learn with a constant effort and application?[1] Is it not delightful to have friends coming from distant quarters?[2] Is it not the Noble Person who feels no displeasure though he falls short of ever achieving recognition?"[3]

ANALECTS I:1

2 □ Confucius' Humanity

There are a number of passages in the *Analects* that give us hints about Confucius' personality. We find out what sort of person Confucius was and the degree to which his personality bore out his teachings. Confucius insisted that a person's words and deeds must match each other. The way Confucius acts, his preferences and his prejudices, are the best clue to not just who he was but also to what he thought and taught.

In these teachings, as in so many other religious traditions, there is an assumption of direct correlation between thought and action. You do not simply hold a certain idea; more important you act upon it and behave in ways that are compatible with the thought. Think of the dictum "Do as I say, not as I do." Can you imagine the Buddha or Jesus reiterating this phrase?

[1] A constant theme in Confucius' discussion of the Noble Person is that the Noble Person lacks bitterness or remorse that others do not recognize his talents. Here the sentiment is expressed by Confucius when he says that he is not troubled should he remain unrecognized. Instead, he would only be troubled if he were unable to recognize the talents of others. Humbly suggesting that recognition of himself by others is of no importance, Confucius goes on to describe his own commitment to finding the talents in others and to working with them in nurturing and developing those talents. Always a teacher of others and yet a humble student himself!

[2] This is one of the most famous statements by Confucius about his view of himself, his learning, and the sages of antiquity. Confucius is suggesting that he views his role as simply the transmission of the learning of the sages of antiquity, rather than the creation of a teaching on his own part. He is seen in this passage as humbly and self-effacingly suggesting that he has contributed nothing to this learning. While such an appraisal is far from the truth, given the creativity with which Confucius approaches the teachings of the sages, nonetheless, it has been characteristic of the tradition as a whole to claim his only contribution is that of transmission.

[3] P'eng is always referenced as the Methuselah of China in ancient times and thus regarded as someone who because of his age would have knowledge of olden times. Confucius is comparing himself to P'eng because P'eng could be seen as a transmitter of the knowledge of the past.

The Master said, "I will not be troubled at people not knowing me; I will be troubled that I do not know people."[1]

ANALECTS I:16

The Master said, "A transmitter and not a maker, believing in and loving the ancients,[2] I venture to compare myself to our old P'eng."[3]

ANALECTS VII:1

4 Given the seriousness of Confucius' teachings and the chaos of his own time, it was important for his disciples to note that he could take his ease, presumably in the company of others. The passage is deceptively simple, but it reinforces the importance of Confucius' emphasis upon life itself, not an escape from it. This teaching finds its fulfillment in human company and the joy of life itself, in the belief that human relationships are the basis for the goodness of all humankind and that the sages themselves realized this in word and deed.

5 This is a revealing statement about Confucius' constant attention to the sages of antiquity and the importance of their words and deeds as a centering principle to his own life and work. The Duke of Chou was one of the founders of the Chou Dynasty (1045–256 BCE) and the epitome of sagely wisdom for Confucius. The passage suggests that Confucius believes that when he is properly focused on learning, even his dreams will include the sages of antiquity. In typical humility, however, he points to his failure to dream of the Duke of Chou as a failure in his attention to and focus on his learning.

6 Here is a suggestion of the practice of proper ritual or propriety, *li*, as well as goodness, *jen*. Confucius restrains himself in eating to extend his sympathy to the individual who has experienced grief in his life. This could also be interpreted in terms of the teaching of reciprocity or empathy, *shu*. As such, the passage suggests the manner in which Confucius embodies his own teachings by how he interacts with those around him.

When the Master was dwelling at ease, his manner was easy, and he looked pleased.[4]

ANALECTS VII:4

The Master said, "Extreme is my decay. For a long time, I have not dreamed, as I was wont to do, that I saw the Duke of Chou."[5]

ANALECTS VII:5

When the Master was eating by the side of a mourner, he never ate to the full.[6]

ANALECTS VII:9

7 This very beautiful statement is often quoted or alluded to by later Confucians suggesting the joys of not just the simple life, but even the life of poverty when grounded in learning and moral principles. The passage draws a clear distinction between the purity of life when pursued with a heart of moral goodness and the life of wealth and honors that have been garnered through means that are not grounded in righteousness. It suggests that a person can endure deprivation and poverty and yet still find happiness when he pursues the path of the sage. As in the teachings of the Buddha and Jesus, the focus is on putting aside worldly possessions and finding the true self. Riches and honors are a false and transient goal, like floating clouds when compared to the foundation of the self obtained through the teaching of righteousness, *i*.

8 The Duke of She is either a local official or an adventurer with little claim to any title, and seen as someone with little understanding of Confucius' teachings.

9 Tzu-lu is one of the most frequently mentioned of Confucius' disciples, a very early follower and potentially the eldest of the group. He was one of the ten disciples known for particular accomplishments, specifically for his skill in governmental affairs. Confucius was often very critical of him, particularly for his rash and reckless courage.

10 Confucius thinks of himself only in terms of his zeal for and commitment to learning. When something larger than yourself occupies your attention, then the matters that drag us all down, even our own advancing years, no longer have any effect.

The Master said, "With coarse rice to eat, with water to drink, and my bended arm for a pillow, I still have joy amid these things. Riches and honors acquired by unrighteousness are to me as a floating cloud."[7]

ANALECTS VII:15

The Duke of She[8] asked Tzu-lu[9] about Confucius, and Tzu-lu did not answer him. The Master said, "Why did you not say to him, 'He is simply a man, who in his eager pursuit *of knowledge* forgets his food, who in his joy *of its attainment* forgets his sorrows, and who does not perceive that old age is coming on?'"[10]

ANALECTS VII:18

11 Here Confucius is shown drawing limits upon how he will conduct himself, suggesting that using a net in fishing or shooting a bird at rest would be to take unfair advantage. His teachings are not a code of nonviolence or harmlessness, nor has the Confucian tradition ever emphasized such moral constrictions, but it does say that humans have ethical responsibilities toward other forms of life, an attitude found in varying degrees from a sense of union with all life in the monism of Buddhism or Hinduism to a sense of stewardship in the theism of Judaism and Christianity. Such an attitude prevails throughout the history of the Confucian tradition. The attitude stems from the moral goodness that is a basic part of any human, and it sees the exercise of that goodness as not limited to humans alone. Confucians respect other forms of life and treat them with a degree of fairness if not kindness.

12 Confucian tradition focuses on the importance of shared human experience. Meaning is found in human company, not in the eremitic ideal of rustication. While not at the level of religious commandments for community, the emphasis on shared experience reiterates what Confucius saw as the paradigmatic role played by the sages of antiquity. Their community embodied these ideals and thus it is appropriate that we attempt to recreate such a community. Learning is not only following the path of the sages of antiquity, but is also to be found within the context of human life itself, that is, shared life with others. Every relationship, every interaction becomes an opportunity for learning and for realizing the moral goodness that lies within and between all of us. What better way to demonstrate this feature of learning than in the joy of singing with your compatriots! And of course there is humor in the passage as well, for Confucius really only wants the song repeated and to join in if the singer can carry a tune!

The Master angled, but did not use a net. He shot, but not at birds perching.[11]

ANALECTS VII:26

When the Master was in company with a person who was singing, if he sang well, he would make him repeat the song, while he accompanied it with his own voice.[12]

ANALECTS VII:31

13 Confucius distinguishes himself from either the sage or the person of goodness, again characterizing himself only as one who focuses all his attention, his total concentration, and his will on the teachings of the sages and never tires of teaching others of the goal.

14 Kung-hsi Hua was a disciple of Confucius said to have been responsible for overseeing Confucius' funeral arrangements and rituals. He admits just how difficult the ideals extolled by Confucius are to embody and exemplify.

15 Here is a set of distinguishing characteristics of Confucius' personality. In each case one characteristic is counterbalanced by another, avoiding extremes. It is as if the ideal is the mean or the middle ground. The sense of the Noble Person is therefore not to be found only in the characteristics that set such a figure apart from others, but also in the very human qualities that draw him toward others. Of the Master it may then be said that he loomed above others, and yet he shared his common humanity with all.

16 Along with the earlier selection in *Analects* VII:26, this is one of the few passages where Confucius refers to—or as the case may be, does not refer to—animals, but only to humans. The passage is most often interpreted as suggesting the priority that Confucius places upon humans in terms of ethical responsibilities. So while he is concerned about whether anyone was burned in the fire in the stable, he does not inquire about the horses. Given that his first priority is learning and the development of moral goodness for humans, it is not a surprising statement; however, it can easily be misinterpreted to suggest that Confucius has no concern for animals. It is not that he has no concern for animals, because there is a larger sphere of moral responsibilities for all life, but he expresses a moral priority for human life.

The Master said, "The Sage and the person of goodness; how dare I *rank myself with them?* It may simply be said of me that I strive to become such without satiety, and teach others without weariness."[13] Kung-hsi Hua said, "This is just what we, the disciples, cannot imitate you in."[14]

ANALECTS VII:33

The Master was mild, and yet dignified; majestic, and yet not fierce; respectful, and yet easy.[15]

ANALECTS VII:37

The stable being burned down when he was at court, on his return the Master said, "Has any person been hurt?" He did not ask about the horses.[16]

ANALECTS X:12

17 All disciples of Confucius. On Tzu-lu and Kung-hsi Hua, see earlier selections in *Analects* VII:18 and VII:33, respectively. Tseng Hsi, also known as Tseng Tian, a minor disciple of Confucius, was the father of Tseng-tzu, a prominent disciple. Jan Yu is associated with issues of government.

18 Confucius' comment is an attempt to minimize the age difference between himself and his disciples in order to equalize the basis of the conversation. Without age difference they are all talking almost as friends and can thus reveal their inner thoughts and not be concerned with the maintenance of the propriety represented by the relation of master and disciple.

19 Confucius' reference to his disciples being "not known" means simply that they have not established their reputations and are thus not known in society or by the political leadership of the time.

20 Personal name for Jan Yu.

21 Measurement of a third of a mile.

22 Personal name for Kung-hsi Hua.

23 A reference to standard robes worn in this case by minor officials.

24 Personal name for Tseng Hsi.

Tzu-lu, Tseng Hsi, Jan Yu, and Kung-hsi Hua[17] were sitting by the Master. He said to them, "Though I am a day or so older than you, do not think of that.[18] From day to day you are saying, 'We are not known.' If some *ruler* were to know you,[19] what would you like to do?" Tzu-lu hastily and lightly replied, "Suppose the case of a state of ten thousand chariots; let it be straitened between *other* large states; let it be suffering from invading armies; and to this there be added a famine in corn and in all vegetables: if I were entrusted with the government of it, in three years' time I could make the people to be bold, and to recognize the rules of righteous conduct." The Master smiled at him. *Turning to Jan Yu he said,* "Ch'iu,[20] what are your wishes?" Ch'iu replied, "Suppose a state of sixty or seventy *li*[21] square, or one of fifty or sixty, and let me have the government of it; in three years' time, I could have plenty to abound among the people. As to *teaching them* the principles of propriety, and music, I must wait for the rise of the Noble Person *to do that.*" "What are your wishes, Ch'ih?"[22] *said the Master next to Kung-hsi Hua.* Ch'ih replied, "I do not say that my ability extends to these things, but I should wish to learn them. At the services of the ancestral temple, and at the audiences of the princes with the sovereign, I should like, dressed in the dark square-made robe[23] and the black linen cap, to act as a small assistant." *Last of all the Master asked Tseng Hsi,* "Tien,[24] what are your wishes?" *Tien,* pausing as he was playing on his lute, while

(continued on page 19)

25 This passage is always quoted to suggest Confucius' true desires. When he asks each of these four disciples his goals, it is not the mission of saving the world that seems closest to his own heart. Where the first three disciples in turn speak of their intended goal to assume a position of rank in various states, and through that process to rectify the ways of the world and return to the ways of the sages, it is only the fourth disciple, whose goals lie outside that mission, who wins Confucius' approval. Although it would seem that undue attention is given to the responses of the first three disciples, particularly when Confucius himself does not share their goals, the importance of their answers lies in the degree to which their goals actually fulfill the intended consequences of Confucius' teachings!

It is not that Tien does not have the same goals as the first three disciples, but he does not state his goal as such and thus can give a very human response to Confucius' question. The very fact that he expresses his joy in life itself communicates to Confucius that he and he alone actually understands the way in which a person lives day to day with the goal of the path of the sage. Perhaps Tien is thus the rightful next ruler.

it was yet sounding, laid the instrument aside and rose. "My wishes," he said, "are different from the cherished purpose of these three gentlemen." "What harm is there in that?" said the Master. "Do you also as well as they speak out your wishes?" *Tien* then said, "In *this* the last month of spring, with the dress of the season all complete, along with five or six young men who have assumed the cap, and six or seven boys, I would wash in the River I, enjoy the breeze among the rain altars, and return home singing." The Master heaved a sigh and said, "I give my approval to Tien."[25]

ANALECTS XI:25

3 □ The Noble Person

The Noble Person, *chün tzu*, represents the highest ideal that Confucius sought to articulate to his disciples and his students. He saw in the Noble Person the closest embodiment of the path of the sage that he felt humankind was capable of attaining. Though far short of the ideal of the sages, figures from antiquity whose words and deeds recorded in the Classics or Confucian scripture most emulated the Way of Heaven, the Noble Person became the embodiment and representation of all Confucian virtues.

We might compare the Noble Person to the saint of Western traditions or the guru or enlightened master of Eastern traditions. However, not everyone has the intention to emulate and become a saint or a guru. In the case of the Confucian tradition, while no one will claim that he has achieved the ideal of the Noble Person, let alone the sage, it remains a goal toward which a person strives, not simply a goal venerated in the attainment of others. In the later periods of Confucianism, or Neo-Confucianism, however, this goal shifts to that of the sage, *sheng*, itself.

1 The term translated as "tool" can also be rendered as "utensil"—both describe the antithesis of what Confucius suggests as the character of the Noble Person. A tool or utensil plays no role in deciding how it might be used by others. It can do good in the right hands, but it can also do evil. The Noble Person determines what is good and acts upon it. In modern parlance, to call someone a tool is to suggest that he will do anything someone asks of him to win favor. This meaning is very close to Confucius' use of the term! How many of us can say that we always stand on our own and that we are not a tool in the hands of others?

2 Tzu-kung, one of Confucius' major disciples, is praised for his skill with language. He is said to have held various government posts. Confucius suggests that perhaps his skill with language lacked an equal accomplishment with goodness.

3 The Noble Person is concerned about the relation between words and deeds. The passage has even been translated to suggest that the Noble Person practices what he preaches and only then preaches what he practices. The Noble Person's integrity is ultimately based on his actions.

4 The Noble Person looks at things from their largest perspective, from the way in which they fit into the whole, and as such he is not partisan or prejudiced. The petty person, on the other hand, can only see the specific item or the specific act and has no comprehension of the broader context into which all things fit. The allusion is to the Noble Person's ability to understand the perspective of the sage, in itself a universal perspective, and thus the Way of Heaven encompassing all things.

The Master said, "The Noble Person is not a tool."[1]

ANALECTS II:12

Tzu-kung[2] asked what constituted the Noble Person. The Master said, "The Noble Person acts before speaking and afterwards speaks according to his actions."[3]

ANALECTS II:13

The Master said, "The Noble Person is broad-minded and not prejudiced. The petty person is prejudiced and not broad-minded."[4]

ANALECTS II:14

5 The passage utilizes the word *tao*, translated as "Way" and generally understood in a broad sense of the Way as, for example, the Way of the Taoists or the Way of the Confucians. Here the term appears in a very specific context as *ch'i tao*—rendered as "the proper way." The implication is that the proper way refers specifically to the moral teachings of the sages and the anticipated goal that the Noble Person would fulfill.

6 It is generally considered that there is a textual problem with this line, and in its present form it seems almost counterintuitive in some translations. The meaning is that if poverty and meanness cannot be put aside by appropriate means, then they should not be avoided. The way of the Noble Person, following the path of the sage, does not necessarily conform to what people most desire. To uphold the ideal of moral goodness may call the person to a life of self-sacrifice.

7 The passage then focuses on the central teaching of goodness, *jen*, suggesting that the Noble Person does not separate himself from this teaching even for a moment. Even in moments of great haste or unusual danger, goodness remains as a compass point of stability from which the Noble Person takes all direction and maintains his course.

8 The Noble Person is unwavering in his commitment to what is righteous or right, *i*. His character of goodness prevails regardless of the shifting winds of the ways of the world. To be for or against things in the world is to be without a defined character, to be subject to the whims and fancies of the changing nature of worldly things. The Noble Person is not detached from the world, but rather he is *in* the world with his feet firmly planted in moral correctness and his path clearly defined by the words and deeds of the sages.

The Master said, "Wealth and honors are what all people desire. If they cannot be obtained in the proper way,[5] they should not be held. Poverty and meanness are what all people dislike. If it cannot be accomplished in the proper way, they should not be avoided.[6] If the Noble Person abandons goodness, how can he fulfill the requirements of that name? The Noble Person does not, even for the space of a single meal, act contrary to goodness. In moments of haste, he cleaves to it. In seasons of danger, he cleaves to it."[7]

ANALECTS IV:5

The Master said, "The Noble Person in the world does not set himself either for things or against things; he simply follows what is right."[8]

ANALECTS IV:10

9 The Noble Person is focused upon *te*, translated as "virtue," where the petty person seeks only the life of worldly enjoyments. This word *te* is central in much of Chinese philosophical writing. For the Confucian, the term suggests moral virtue and reflects the way of the sages and the embodiment of Heaven.

10 The Confucian sense of following the law is not legalistic, but based on moral principles rather than the bestowment of special favors. Thus a Noble Person does not seek special treatment, perks, or political favors. The message is clear that this is not a person who will be subject to worldly influence.

11 Confucius contrasts one of his most important teachings, *i*, righteousness or rightness, with profit, *li*. Its core meaning as righteousness or rightness essentially defines a process of self-understanding. Self-understanding manifests the moral character of the individual or the capacity for righteousness.

  The Noble Person's actions are for the benefit of all persons, not selfish aggrandizement for personal ends. The distinction between righteousness and profit will be famously utilized by Mencius (ca. fourth century BCE), Confucius' principal later interpreter. Mencius will suggest to a ruler of the day that rather than focusing on profit, he should spend all his energy trying to implement *jen*, goodness, and *i*, righteousness.

12 The Noble Person's words reflect careful thought and consideration. He is sensitive to the feelings of others, but this is not a sign of weakness. Nor should it be concluded that he is not a person of action. Confucius emphasizes that the Noble Person is extraordinarily kind, but is also a person of untold strength in his commitment to take action on the basis of establishing what is righteous.

The Master said, "The Noble Person cherishes virtue; the petty person cherishes comfort;[9] the Noble Person cherishes the law; the petty person cherishes favors."[10]

ANALECTS IV:11

The Master said, "The Noble Person is conversant with righteousness; the petty person is conversant with profit."[11]

ANALECTS IV:16

The Master said, "The Noble Person is cautious in his words, but deliberate in his actions."[12]

ANALECTS IV:24

13 A minister in the state of Cheng during Confucius' life whom Confucius admired.

14 The reference to the Noble Person in Chinese reads "the Way of the Noble Person," emphasizing the degree to which Confucius is defining a Way for the Noble Person.

15 What Legge has translated as respectful is the term *ching*, serious or reverential, and suggests the solemnity with which Confucius held superiors, an attitude no different from that with which he held the sages of the past.

16 "Just" translates *i*, rightness or righteousness, and suggests more than mere justice. The word reveals a level of self-understanding of moral goodness and thus the application of that goodness to the interactions with and governing of all people.

The Master said of Tzu-ch'an[13] that he possessed four
of the characteristics of the Noble Person:[14] In his
conduct of himself, he was humble; in serving his
superiors, he was respectful;[15] in nourishing the people,
he was kind; in ordering the people, he was just.[16]

ANALECTS V:15

17 "Raw nature," *chih*, means essentially the material nature or disposition of the person without cultivation or learning.

18 Culture, *wen*, is a key term for Confucius and may be translated as "literature," where it is understood broadly to refer to the pursuits of individuals who engage in learning and study.

19 Too much raw nature will only produce a rustic, that is, someone who would have no use for the process of learning and study. This is no surprise, considering the emphasis that Confucius places on study and learning.

20 The surprise is Confucius' criticism of the possibility of an excess of *wen*. While the acquisition of *wen* is important, too much *wen* is also a danger and its outcome is not positive. The term for "pedant" essentially means someone who takes learning as an end unto itself and thus does not see the degree to which *wen* must be put into the larger context of the whole person, not just intellectual development.

21 For the person who has fulfilled his nature, learning is the result of his ability to achieve a balance between the raw nature and the culture that is added. The path of the sage doesn't disregard the material nature we are made of; at the same time, it does not overemphasize the capacity for the inculcation of learning. The Noble Person finds a balance of the two, or the mean in which both are recognized for their capacity to fulfill the nature of what it means to be human.

22 *Tang*, "calm and composed," means essentially to be at peace and suggests the degree to which the Noble Person is at peace with his life. For the petty person the opposite condition prevails—he is constantly agitated and nervous, *ch'i*. Without the perspective of the Noble Person, there is only insecurity in ever-changing conditions, with no centering principle to hold on to. Without the focus of the Noble Person, no peace will be found in life.

The Master said, "Where raw nature[17] is in excess of culture,[18] we have rusticity;[19] where culture is in excess of raw nature, we have the manners of a pedant.[20] When culture and raw nature are equally blended, we then have the Noble Person."[21]

ANALECTS VI:16

The Master said, "The Noble Person is calm and composed; the petty person is anxious and distressed."[22]

ANALECTS VII:36

23 Otherwise known as Ssu-ma Kang or Li Kang, a native of the state of Sung and considered a disciple of Confucius.

24 Confucius explains why there is no fear or anxiety in the character of the Noble Person: in the process of self-reflection or self-examination, he finds no faults within himself. He is not self-righteous; rather, finding his inner nature brings him into accord with the path of the sage and thus with the Way of Heaven. Confucius will repeatedly hearken back to a process of self-reflection as the basis for establishing the sense of self. With this process, often called self-cultivation, comes a sense of peace and calm. Similarly, in numerous religious traditions, meditation, contemplation, and prayer play key roles in reducing anxiety by defining the self within a larger context of ultimate meaning.

25 In your interactions with others, you can either bring out their best or their worst qualities. Beginning with the perspective that everyone has admirable qualities that can be nurtured and developed, the Noble Person works to help each person develop such qualities to the full range of his capabilities. The Noble Person also understands that should this moral nature not be developed, humans are capable of evil. The petty person will exploit this potential for evil and with it will develop the world as we largely know it, a world that chooses to turn against goodness in the name of personal gain, selfishness, and worldly pleasures.

26 While there is collegiality, friendship, and warmth in the character of the Noble Person, there is not a display of excessive praise in a maudlin fashion suggesting the behavior of the sycophant. The key is respect and dignity, demonstrating honest and truthful feelings. A simple statement, but perhaps not such a simple virtue to emulate!

Ssu-ma Niu[23] asked about the Noble Person. The Master said, "The Noble Person has neither anxiety nor fear." "Being without anxiety or fear!" said Niu. "Does this constitute what we call the Noble Person?" The Master said, "When interior examination discovers nothing wrong, what is there is to be anxious about, what is there to fear?"[24]

ANALECTS XII:4

The Master said, "The Noble Person *seeks to* perfect the admirable qualities of people, and does not *seek to* perfect their bad qualities. The petty person does the opposite of this."[25]

ANALECTS XII:16

The Master said, "The Noble Person is affable, but not adulatory; the petty person is adulatory, but not affable."[26]

ANALECTS XIII:23

27 It is easy to mistake a dignified air, especially when a person is at ease, as a mark of pride and arrogance. Confucius has something else in mind, suggesting that the Noble Person by his learning and self-examination has developed an outward appearance reflecting the inward sense of peace and calm found in the realization of goodness. Such an appearance is not to be mistaken for the banal sense of the petty person whose countenance bears pride without the foundation of dignity.

28 While there have been differences of interpretation as to whether the passage is suggesting a movement upwards or higher understanding versus its opposite, the passage is clear in distinguishing an intention toward that which is higher and that which is lower.

29 The Noble Person again shows his reluctance to boast or brag, remaining self-effacing and humble in any discussion of accomplishments. However, he demonstrates his commitment, devotion, and ability to achieve results. Far better to act than to talk and far better to remain modest about what might be accomplished.

The Master said, "The Noble Person has a dignified ease without pride. The petty person has pride without dignified ease."[27]

ANALECTS XIII:26

The Master said, "The progress of the Noble Person is upwards; the progress of the petty person is downwards."[28]

ANALECTS XIV:24

The Master said, "The Noble Person is modest in his speech, but exceeds in his actions."[29]

ANALECTS XIV:29

30 Confucius describes these three attributes of the Noble Person as the Way, *tao*, of the Noble Person, suggesting the degree to which they compose basic attributes of the figure, and humbly suggests his own distance from these qualities.

31 The first attribute of the Noble Person is the virtue of *jen*, goodness or humaneness, and suggests again the centrality of this virtue to all that makes up and defines the Noble Person.

32 The term for "wise," *chih*, suggests knowledge, but gives that knowledge a status that makes the Noble Person free of perplexities or doubts. This knowledge is nothing short of the knowledge of the path of the sage itself.

33 See earlier selection in *Analects* II:13.

34 Tzu-kung suggests that the description given of the Noble Person is precisely the nature of the way of the Master himself.

The Master said, "The way[30] of the Noble Person is threefold, but I am not equal to it. As a person of goodness,[31] he is free from anxieties; wise,[32] he is free from perplexities; bold, he is free from fear. Tzu-kung[33] said, "Master, that is what you yourself say!"[34]

ANALECTS XIV:30

35 See *Analects* VII:18 (chapter 2).

36 "Cultivation of himself," *hsiu chi*, or in its more common form *hsiu shen* from Mencius, will become known in the Confucian tradition as "self-cultivation," the principal means of learning through interior focus. It will suggest to later Confucians the cultivation of the heart/mind, *hsin*, as well as the nature, *hsing*, and often will be described in terms of the cultivation of a state of *ching*, seriousness or reverence, which is rendered here as "reverential carefulness," and suggests a heightened awareness focused upon your nature and the correspondence between that nature and the path of the sage.

37 "Rest," *an*, also means peace. Confucius uses this term in deep and profound ways. He suggests in *Analects* IV:2, for example, that he comes to "rest" in *jen*, goodness, postulating a sense of an ultimate peace highly significant in terms of religious meaning. Here he suggests that such rest or peace comes to the people as a product of the Noble Person's own self-cultivation and manifestation of goodness.

38 The reference to two sages of antiquity, Yao and Shun, suggests that the Noble Person's accomplishment in cultivating himself would receive the accolade of the sages themselves.

Tzu-lu[35] asked what constituted the Noble Person. The Master said, "The cultivation of himself in reverential carefulness."[36] "And is this all?" said *Tzu-lu*. "He cultivates himself so as to give rest to others,"[37] was the reply. "And is this all?" *again* asked *Tzu-lu*. *The Master* said, "He cultivates himself so as to give rest to all the people. He cultivates himself so as to give rest to all the people— even Yao and Shun were still solicitous about this."[38]

ANALECTS XIV:45

39 Confucius is placing the virtue of righteousness or rightness, *i*, as central to his teaching and to the character of the Noble Person. The core meaning of righteousness remains the sense of inner self-understanding.

40 Righteousness is seen as the core to the performance of rites or the attitude of propriety, *li*. Rites or propriety are always discussed by Confucius as more than simply the correct performance of the rites or the correct attitude of propriety. They are instead a matter of inner feelings, not just outward performance.

41 The depth of self-understanding, a measure of progress on the path of the sage, can only manifest itself in humility because the self has realized a greater capacity than itself, the Way of Heaven, and as such there is no room left for the pettiness of arrogance.

42 Sincerity, *ch'eng*, is one of the most important teachings in the Confucian tradition, particularly in the work *Chung Yung*, the *Doctrine of the Mean* (ca. 200–0 BCE), one of the most subtle and abstract of early writings highlighted by the Confucian tradition. Sincerity or integrity suggests being true to yourself and thus to others. The depth of self-understanding underlying your interactions determines what is shown to others.

43 The Noble Person's only concern is with his own learning and self-cultivation, not the reputation that may follow him or for that matter may elude him. Have we created a world that shares in these goals of the Noble Person?

44 Confucius emphasizes the need to look within. There are multiple possible interpretations of this very brief statement, but they all highlight the primacy of an internal process of reflection, learning, and self-cultivation. This statement strongly stresses taking responsibility for your actions. By contrast, the petty person can only look toward others. He has no self-reflection and does not assume responsibility for his actions.

The Master said, "The Noble Person considers righteousness to be essential.[39] He performs it according to the rules of propriety.[40] He brings it forth in humility.[41] He completes it with sincerity.[42] This is indeed the Noble Person."

ANALECTS XV:17

The Master said, "The Noble Person is distressed by his want of ability. He is not distressed by others not knowing him."[43]

ANALECTS XV:18

The Master said, "What the Noble Person seeks is in himself. What the petty person seeks is in others."[44]

ANALECTS XV:20

45 The Noble Person remains dignified regardless of circumstances and does not contend, argue, or engage in disputation. He interacts with others and welcomes human contact. He is not, after all, a recluse! His interactions, however, show the strength of his character. He remains free from cliques, free from the pettiness that divides people, and thus can bring them together for the good of a common cause.

46 The term translated by Legge as "truth" is Way, *tao*. "Truth" accurately conveys the sense of ultimate meaning that the Noble Person finds in the process of learning. In this particular passage the Way is nothing less than truth for Confucius, and thus the Confucian Way.

47 The comparison between learning and food suggests that both in learning and in farming it is quite possible that you will come up wanting for nourishment. While the pursuit of learning may result in poverty, that option is preferred to having food but no learning. The Noble Person's anxiety is centered on the quest for learning, not on the particular physical conditions that might be produced by a life devoted only to learning. To pursue learning occasions sacrifice and often results in enforced poverty, but poverty is a small price to pay in the pursuit of truth.

48 To simply be firm is potentially to be of narrow mind, to be rigid, unbending, and unable to understand the consequences of such firmness. To be correctly firm, however, is to ground the firmness in the understanding of moral goodness; the firmness then sets the direction for the implementation of goodness. Such firmness yields not to temptation, to the ways of the world, or to the ways of the petty person because it is focused on what is good from the outset.

49 This passage and the next seem to go together; in the first case are three things the Noble Person guards against, and the next three are things of which the Noble Person stands in awe. Whether it be the lust of youth, the stubbornness of middle age, or the desire to possess that comes with old age, the Noble Person is to be vigilant of these potential faults throughout his life.

The Master said, "The Noble Person is dignified, but does not wrangle. He is sociable, but not a partisan."[45]

ANALECTS XV:21

The Master said, "The object of the Noble Person is truth.[46] Food is not his object. There is plowing; even in that there is *sometimes* want. So with learning; emolument may be found in it. The Noble Person is anxious lest he should not get truth; he is not anxious lest poverty should come upon him."[47]

ANALECTS XV:31

The Master said, "The Noble Person is correctly firm, and not firm merely."[48]

ANALECTS XV:36

Confucius said, "There are three things that the Noble Person guards against. In youth when the physical powers are not yet settled, he guards against lust. When he is strong, and the physical powers are full of vigor, he guards against quarrelsomeness. When he is old, and the physical powers are decayed, he guards against covetousness."[49]

ANALECTS XVI:7

50   The ordinances of Heaven, *T'ien-ming*, is the term for the Mandate of Heaven, the ruler's sanction on the basis of the authority granted to him by Heaven. Some commentators have chosen to see in this expression, however, not so much the traditional basis of rule, as rather the moral nature of the individual given by Heaven to humankind. Whether individual or societal, power and authority in human culture are found in Heaven. Great men are those who have been raised up by Heaven to rule humankind. Finally, to complement the power and authority bestowed by Heaven, Confucius recognizes the words of the sages as an embodiment of the authority of Heaven and thus stands in awe of them. The passage as a whole suggests the degree to which the Noble Person, by recognizing these sources of awe, expresses his religious response to the ultimate authority, Heaven, *T'ien*, the basis of the religious foundation of the Confucian tradition.

51   Summarizing the general character of the Noble Person, Confucius covers most areas of conduct and action that would be involved for any of us in living each day. The Noble Person is sensitized to each and every thought and action as part of the larger context of learning. All thoughts and actions must be examined to ensure that they are in accord with learning itself, that is, with the words and the deeds of the sages. The overarching teaching of the entire passage, the governing principle of righteousness, *i*, suggests that all thought and action must be held in the clarity of righteousness, the fulfillment of self-understanding, and thus the capacity to inculcate goodness into every moment of each day.

Confucius said, "There are three things of which the Noble Person stands in awe. He stands in awe of the ordinances of Heaven. He stands in awe of great men. He stands in awe of the words of the sages."[50]

ANALECTS XVI:8

Confucius said, "The Noble Person has nine things that are subjects of thoughtful consideration. In regard to the use of his eyes, he is anxious to see clearly. In regard to the use of his ears, he is anxious to hear distinctly. In regard to his countenance, he is anxious that it should be benign. In regard to his demeanor, he is anxious that it should be respectful. In regard to his speech, he is anxious that it should be sincere. In regard to his affairs, he is anxious that they should be serious. In regard to what he doubts about, he is anxious to question others. When he is angry, he thinks of the difficulties he might cause others. When he sees gain to be got, he thinks of righteousness."[51]

ANALECTS XVI:10

52 See *Analects* VII:18 (chapter 2).

53 Confucius distinguishes between bravery and moral persuasion. When asked whether the Noble Person is brave, the response is that righteousness, *i*, moral persuasion, is of much greater importance than bravery. That is not to say that the Noble Person is not brave. He will in fact stand for righteousness whenever necessary, regardless of the danger in which he might place himself or the potential resulting sacrifice. Such actions, however, are motivated by righteousness, not by bravery alone. He then suggests the problems that are created by prioritizing bravery. Rather than commit such errors, the Noble Person knows that action must always be governed by moral goodness.

54 See earlier selection in *Analects* II:13.

55 The Noble Person has feelings just like anyone else, and there are things that he is passionate about. In like manner, there are things that he abhors and hates, believing that certain types of conduct and certain attitudes are contrary to the goal of learning, the path of the sage, and the Way of Heaven.

Confucius does not teach universal love of everyone and everything. However, that which is not good is not wantonly destroyed or eliminated, but rather transformed into that which is good. This attitude reflects Confucius' enormous optimism in the ability of humans not only to learn but also to become good. Do we have such optimism?

Tzu-lu[52] said, "Does the Noble Person esteem valor?" The Master said, "The Noble Person holds righteousness to be of highest importance. A Noble Person having valor without righteousness will be guilty of insubordination; the petty person having valor without righteousness will commit robbery."[53]

ANALECTS XVII:23

Tzu-kung[54] said, "Has the Noble Person his hatreds also?" The Master said, "He has his hatreds. He hates those who proclaim the evil of others. He hates the man who, being in a low station, slanders his superiors. He hates those who have valor *merely*, and are unobservant of propriety. He hates those who are forward and determined, and, *at the same time*, of contracted understanding."[55]

ANALECTS XVII:24

4 □ On Filial Piety

There is probably no more universally known virtue generally associated with East and Southeast Asian cultures and Confucianism specifically than that of filial piety, a phrase suggesting the relation of parents and children and frequently associated with a sense of extraordinary obligation of the children toward their parents. However, something rather different than mere obligation is meant by the term when used by Confucius.

The term itself, *hsiao*, is composed of two parts, one signifying a child and the other a contracted form of the character for "old man." Thus the word literally indicates the relationship between child and parent. Confucius calls attention not so much to the obligation between parent and child, as rather a heartfelt feeling of mutual love and respect. The feelings themselves are of greatest concern to Confucius because they reflect the goodness that Confucius focuses upon as his central teaching.

It is important to understand that this relation is built upon the moral actions of the parents toward their children. The responsibility of the parents toward their children is seen in three important ways. First, there is the simple biological fact that an infant is helpless and will not survive without nurturing and care. This is the first responsibility of the parent toward the child. Second, the child cannot become a moral person without proper education of mind and heart. This is the role of learning and the second responsibility of the parent in terms of providing the proper foundation for the child. Third, it is expected that the parents will themselves be the moral example for the child in the home, where the first and most important lessons of moral conduct are learned. However, this ideal set of conditions is not always the case.

1 We begin with a passage that would generally be interpreted as the obligation of the child to the parent, a duty to everything desired by the father both in life and in death. While Confucius may well be trying to show the extent of natural love between parents and children, history often told another tale, one that saw little opportunity for the child to move outside the influence of the parents and whose own life was thus consumed in service to his parents. The unstated assumption of the passage, however, is that the parents are themselves acting in moral ways and it is this moral goodness that is the basis of the son's obedience to their actions.

2 A close disciple of Confucius said to be accomplished in culture or literature, *wen*.

3 The Master's response to the question of the nature of filial piety in his own day is harsh. What he observes is care and support, but no feeling. He says that even animals take care of their own kind and asks if there is not something with which we might differentiate human conduct from animal behavior. The answer lies in the attitude here described as reverence, *ching*. It is the human who can provide care with a sense of the moral relation that exists between people.

4 A close disciple of Confucius known like Tzu-yu for his knowledge of culture or literature, *wen*, though he is particularly associated with book learning.

5 There is some complexity with the interpretation of this sentence. Translator D. C. Lau takes it to mean the expression of the parent's face; Sinologist Arthur Waley, to mean the demeanor. These interpretations suggest the need to be attentive to the parents' approval or disapproval and thus to their most sensitive needs.

6 To put the issue in contemporary times, do you simply stick your parents in a nursing home and regard that act as a sufficient display of care for them? Confucius stresses again that there should be an expression of a natural love between children and parents, which is the real basis of filial piety, not simply paying the monthly bills!

The Master said, "While a man's father is alive, look at the bent of his will; when his father is dead, look at his conduct. If for three years he does not alter from the way of his father, he may be called filial."[1]

Analects I:11

Tzu-yu[2] asked what filial piety was. The Master said, "The filial piety of nowadays means the support of one's parents. But dogs and horses likewise are able to do something in the way of support; without reverence, what is there to distinguish the one support given from the other?"[3]

Analects II:7

Tzu-hsia[4] asked what filial piety was. The Master said, "The difficulty is with the countenance.[5] If, when *their elders* have any *troublesome* affairs, the young take the toil of them, and if, when *the young* have wine and food, they set them before their elders, is this to be considered filial piety?"[6]

Analects II:8

7 This statement certainly represents a different relationship between parents and children than that experienced in most modern societies. Here the emphasis is on both the seniority of the parents and yet also on the moral responsibility of the child to speak up when he sees something wrong. When the parents refuse his remonstration, then he only shows deeper respect for their status and greater concern for the correction of their ways. Even should this go to a stage of punishment, the son does not give up in his attempt to rectify what he perceives to be wrong. This very behavior is seen as quintessentially demonstrating the deep and profound love between parents and children.

8 With no means of communication and no security, travel was seen as bringing insecurity to parents when they lacked knowledge of the whereabouts of their son as well as the inability to call him home should some emergency arise. Passages like this one are often challenged for taking freedom from the child.

But is this the point of the passage? Is the issue superficially about "staying within reach" or about valuing moral relationships? Likewise, in our own day, when there are more ways to "stay in touch" than could ever be imagined, do we devalue the inner meaning of our relationships through superficial forms of communication?

9 This is a reminder to the filial son that he should be constantly vigilant of his parents' age and condition. He can take joy in their health and well-being, but he can also find anxiety in their age and increasing fragility. The passage reminds the child of the importance of the parents' role in the child's life and suggests that the memories of his parents refer both to their role as moral instructors that he should continue to stand in awe of, as well as their role as loving parents whom he should find joy in.

The Master said, "In serving his parents *a son* may remonstrate with them, but gently: when he sees that they do not incline to follow *his advice*, he shows an increased degree of reverence, but does not abandon *his purpose*; and should they punish him, he does not allow himself to murmur."[7]

ANALECTS IV:18

The Master said, "While his parents are alive, *the son* may not go abroad to a distance. If he does go abroad, he must have a fixed place to which he goes."[8]

ANALECTS IV:19

The Master said, "The age of the parents may by no means not be kept in memory, as an occasion at once for joy and for fear."[9]

ANALECTS IV:21

10   See *Analects* VII:18 (chapter 2).

11   This passage is frequently quoted to demonstrate the difference between Confucian teachings and legalism, a competing school of thought that emphasized law at the expense of all moral relations. The Duke of She is proud of his ability to have enacted what he refers to as uprightness, *chih*, a behavioral code he sees as enforcing the complete honesty of all his citizens. The term "upright" does mean honesty, but for Confucius it implies a moral code. To be upright is to reveal that which is moral within you, and that capacity of inner morality, goodness, will carry with it certain moral behaviors, including the practice of filial piety. So while it might be argued that it is completely honest for a son to report his father if the father has engaged in some dishonest circumstance, the issue revolves around a priority in the special moral relation of filial piety over that of individual uprightness.

To what extent do you shelter wrongdoing? There was no easy answer to this question for Confucius any more than there is today for us. For Confucius the answer lies in the ambiguous interface of honesty and the need to demonstrate filial piety, including the role of the son in remonstrating his parents should he find wrongdoing (see the earlier selection in *Analects* IV:18). The very ambiguity of the issue suggests the relevance for our own time and for our own struggles of conscience.

12   A disciple thought to be someone Confucius felt did not live up to his expectations.

13   After several years of neglect the practices would have been forgotten.

The Duke of She[10] informed Confucius, saying, "Among us here there are those who may be deemed upright in their conduct. If their father has stolen a sheep, they will bear witness to the fact." Confucius said, "Among us, in our part of the country, those who are upright are different from this. The father conceals the misconduct of the son, and the son conceals the misconduct of the father. Uprightness is to be found in this."[11]

ANALECTS XIII:18

Tsai Wo[12] asked about the three years' mourning period *for parents, saying* that one year was long enough. He said, "If the Noble Person abstains for three years from the observances of propriety, those observances will be quite lost.[13] If for three years he abstains from music, music will be quite lost. *Within a year* the old grain is exhausted, and the new grain has sprung up, and, in procuring fire by friction, we go through all the changes of wood for that purpose. After a complete year, the mourning may stop." The Master said, "If you were, *after a year*, to eat good rice, and wear embroidered clothes, would you feel at ease?" "I should," replied Wo. The Master said, "If you can feel at ease, do it. But a Noble Person, during the whole period of mourning, does not enjoy pleasant food that he may eat, nor derive pleasure from music that he may hear. He also does not feel at ease if he is comfortably lodged. Therefore he does not do *what you propose*. But now you feel at ease and may do it." Tsai Wo

(continued on page 57)

14 Tsai Wo's familiar name.

15 Tradition dictated a period of three years' mourning; during that time the restrictions discussed by Tsai Wo would be enacted. Tsai Wo suggests that mourning should be limited to a year, arguing that the cycles of nature are encompassed in a year's period. Confucius clearly disagrees. Once Tsai Wo has left, Confucius expresses his consternation with Tsai Wo's ethical standards, as well as a certain level of sarcasm that Tsai Wo seems intent on *quantifying* his parents' love and care for him.

Confucius' explanation offers a real insight into the nature of filial piety. The length of mourning is tied to the period of the parents' nurturing of their child during the stage of helplessness, without which the child would not survive. This passage is the basis for understanding Confucius' sense of the *reciprocal* nature of filial piety, where there are obligations and responsibilities on the part of both parties. That children should serve their parents is not some slavish obligation because of the seniority of the parents, but rather a reciprocal relation that begins with the care extended by the parents to the children. In our own day and age, I suspect that far too many would find even Tsai Wo's standards too restrictive of their self-interest.

then went out, and the Master said, "This shows Yü's[14] want of virtue. It is not till a child is three years old that it is allowed to leave the arms of its parents. And the three years' mourning is universally observed throughout the empire. Did Yü enjoy the three years' love of his parents?"[15]

ANALECTS XVII:21

5 ☐ Ritual and Music

Confucius came from a society that valued ritual. Conduct and behavior were measured by the ability to know and execute the proper ritual when it was deemed necessary. Given its highly hierarchical structure, society was seen as held together by a set of proper relationships and interactions, what we might describe as ritual enactment of proper relations. Such rituals governed almost all interactions and events of the individual, family, community, and state.

Some material preserved in the largest of the ritual texts, the *Li Chi*, or *Record of Ritual*, suggests a common understanding about the similarity of the meaning of music and ritual, which both play a significant role in Confucian thought. We come away from the *Analects* feeling that music and ritual are a barometer of peace and harmony, of self and society's ability to emulate the ways of the sages of antiquity.

Music and ritual were standards against which Confucius measured the disarray of his time, in a crisis of inner content and inner meaning. Thus Confucius sought a sense of ritual that contained inner reverence and respect and that reflected the order and structure of all things under the authority of Heaven. To perform ritual was to enter into that sphere of order and authority with reverence.

Music in its deeper meaning is no different from ritual in its intention and purpose. It, too, is a symbol for order and harmony, what our classical Greek heritage refers to as the "music of the spheres." To feel music is to enter into the very harmony of the spheres themselves. For Confucius, music and ritual are a direct method of experiencing the order and peace provided by Heaven.

1 The term for goodness is *jen*. Legge's translation renders the term "virtues proper to humanity." Legge seeks to demonstrate the universal nature of *jen* as the essential virtue of Confucian thought.

2 Confucius places propriety, *li*, in juxtaposition to *jen*, goodness. Some will argue that ritual is first and foremost a performative act whose efficacy is a direct product of the accuracy of performance. We know of course that anyone can perform a ritual, but Confucius argues that only the person of goodness may perform the ritual with true meaning and understanding.

3 Confucius brings together the spheres of music and ritual, arguing that both require goodness of character if they are to be meaningful. Music and ritual are complementary and serve a larger goal of a reverential attitude.

In a number of cultures and religious traditions, standards of aesthetic judgment are rooted in moral values, and Confucians have always sought to find moral virtue in a wide range of human activities. Confucius is suggesting the importance of seeing ritual and music as two ways in which ultimate meaning can be brought into the individual's life precisely because each can reflect that deepest character of humankind and the ways of Heaven. Are we so different when we seek to find ultimate meaning in aesthetic expression?

The Master said, "If a person be without the virtues proper to goodness,[1] what has he to do with the rites of propriety?[2] If a person be without the virtues proper to goodness, what has he to do with music?"[3]

ANALECTS III:3

4 A citizen of the state of Lu who is known only by this passage.

5 Festive rituals might include cappings, weddings, or various sacrifices, where the tendency might be toward extravagance and opulent display. Confucius recommends minimum expenditure. To those who would say that only extravagance properly displays your commitment, Confucius suggests that the feelings are entirely separate from the lavishness of the ceremony. In fact, if anything, high expenditures only inhibit the true feelings. Reverence and solemnity are the feelings to be cultivated, not the material display of wealth.

Likewise, Confucius suggests that in mourning rituals it is easy to be swept away with attention to detail and to use such attention as a way of diverting or hiding your true feelings. Yet the true meaning of a mourning ritual has nothing to do with detail. It is instead about feelings of profound sorrow.

Frankly, a number of rituals presented in our own time, either through extravagant displays of wealth or through elaborate performances, convey only a perfunctory sense of inner feeling. Suppose we ourselves consider the relation between all the ritual moments that make up our lives and attempt to see them in the light of propriety—true feelings representing inner feelings of goodness. Does such an insight change the nature of our performances?

Lin Fang[4] asked what was the first thing to be attended to in ritual. The Master said, "A great question indeed! In *festive* rituals it is better to be sparing than extravagant. In rituals of mourning, it is better that there be deep sorrow than a minute attention to detail."[5]

ANALECTS III:4

6 See *Analects* II:13 (chapter 3).

7 The ritual behind this passage concerns the king giving out a calendar for the following year in which his nobles would confirm and request authority for their duties by the ritual sacrifice of a sheep at the beginning of each month. This request for sanction was largely ignored and as a result Tzu-kung thought that the ceremony had become a needless sacrifice.

8 Ssu is Tzu-kung's familiar name. Confucius' response suggests that even though parts of the ritual were ignored, the act of the ritual ought to be retained and maintained. While this passage appears to contradict Confucius' sense of the importance of feeling over performance, what Confucius calls for here is the recognition of the larger context of ritual. This particular ritual set the context for the relation of the various states to the rulers of the Chou Dynasty, and thus for the full reverence for the symbolic power the Chou Dynasty possessed. Through its rulers, the Chou Dynasty embodied the full extent of the power of Heaven itself. The larger and deeper meaning of ritual is the indication of the proper attitude of reverence and a reflection of the order of the self and society.

9 The term Legge translates as "complaisance" can also be rendered as "courtesy" or "decorum." The passage emphasizes a style of leadership or governance in compliance with ritual and suggests that if ritual (or propriety, reverence, and decorum) is the overriding concern, then the state will be well governed. In turn, if the ruler cannot govern with ritual, then he will be unable to govern properly.

Tzu-kung[6] wished to do away with the offering of a sheep connected with the inauguration of the first day of the month.[7] The Master said, "Ssu, you love the sheep; I love the ritual."[8]

ANALECTS III:17

The Master said, "If *a prince* is able to govern his kingdom with the complaisance proper to the rules of propriety, what difficulty will he have? If he cannot govern it with that complaisance, what has he to do with the rules of propriety?"[9]

ANALECTS IV:13

10 This is a reference to the music of the sage king Shun, which was said to be perfect in every respect, that is, perfect harmony as well as perfect feeling or sentiment.

11 This is a statement of Confucius' inability to taste food, not a specific reference to a meat or vegetarian diet.

12 For Confucius, the beauty of music is associated with its moral impact and its ability to inspire both himself and others with greater appreciation of beauty, beauty always associated with moral goodness as embodied by the sages of antiquity. Is this interpretation of music or its potential effects necessarily any different from the transformative effects we might experience through a Bach cantata, a Mozart mass, a Rachmaninoff concerto, or even Keith Jarrett or Pink Floyd?

13 Ritual is more than the objects offered in sacrifice, and music is more than the sound of bells and drums. Both music and ritual, to express their true and profound meanings, represent an attitude, a way of relating to and respecting that which has ultimate meaning. A person assigns ultimate meaning to that which stands above her and encompasses her in a harmony of humankind with Heaven itself. Is it possible that our own ritual behaviors contain the seeds of some deeper mystery and meaning that have the capacity to bring about ultimate self-understanding?

The Christian theologian Paul Tillich talked of this capacity for ultimate meaning as a depth dimension. In his mind, there was not some separate sphere of religious meaning and truth standing apart from all other dimensions of the human spirit. Rather, it was a question of depth, depth that could be found in all forms of human expression. Is Confucius saying anything different?

When the Master was in Ch'i, he heard the Shao[10] and for three months did not know the taste of meat.[11] "I did not think," he said, "that music could have been made so excellent as this."[12]

ANALECTS VII:13

The Master said, "'It is according to the rules of propriety,' they say. 'It is according to the rules of propriety,' they say. Are gems and silk all that is meant by propriety? 'It is music,' they say. 'It is music,' they say. Are bells and drums all that is meant by music?"[13]

ANALECTS XVII:11

6 □ The Nature of Learning

Confucius suggests that the attempt to find meaning, to build true self-understanding, and from this self-understanding, to build a world of mutual respect and goodness, is always grounded in learning. Learning is not just the acquisition of knowledge, but the thorough inward assimilation and application of that knowledge. The process is shared with others, with a learning community. For Confucius, learning always begins with the individual and then extends to others and to the world at large.

Most of the passages in the *Analects* that refer to subjects of learning spell out specific literary sources. Frequent themes of discourse are the Classics of Poetry, History, and Ritual, *shih*, *shu*, and *li*. Through the study of these sources, any person could cultivate their moral nature because of the ultimately pure moral nature of the Classics.

For contemporary readers, these particular sources may seem alien and too specific to Confucius' historical context. However, his specific focus on the Classics did not mean that there was not a very broad foundation for learning at the same time. As specific as *wen*, literature, can be, it can be equally broad—it is culture, it is human relationships, it is the relation of humankind to all things—and all of these aspects came to be regarded as a part of the learning process. Confucius saw the dynamic of learning as stretching through every fiber of life.

People learned to emulate the best in others, as well as to avoid what was less than admirable in them. They learned from human society and from the natural world. Confucius embraces both narrow and broad approaches in his advocacy of learning, celebrating the ability of the human mind to understand the nature of things through the commitment to learning.

1 | Learning is a complete activity of the individual; there is no dichotomy of lifestyle and the undertaking of learning. Simplicity of lifestyle, an intentional non-satiation of the appetites—these characteristics speak to a life of earnestness in the pursuit of a goal thought to be of a higher order.

For a person of true learning, learning is the all-consuming goal and fulfillment of life itself. In the pursuit of that goal mundane and more conventional pursuits are put aside. You seek out people who will further that goal, not compromise it in terms of lesser worldly pursuits. The style of wealth and ease to allow the means and leisure to pursue whatever you fancy is at best inimical to the rigors that Confucius sets for his students.

2 | Confucius contrasts two mental processes, learning, *hsüeh*, and thought, *ssu*. Learning involves the acquisition of knowledge toward the express aim of its implementation in moral action. Thought is part of the process of knowledge acquisition, but it might best be described as the process of reasoning or reflecting that further refines the context of the learning process.

To engage in the acquisition of knowledge without reasoning or reflection is regarded as useless. The raw accumulation of knowledge and its regurgitation is not real knowledge. Do you really know something if you have not reflected and reasoned it thoroughly?

3 | Likewise, Confucius is wary of the exercise of thought alone. Reasoning or reflection must have for Confucius both *content* and *intent*. If there is no content and therefore no intent, then it does not further the goals of the learning agenda. You can't get to the process of developing the moral nature, let alone the implementation of moral action, if there is nothing upon which this capacity of thought is focused. It is simply an empty process, and it is perilous because it ends with nothing, or worse, it ends in a failure to pursue what should be the true nature of learning.

The Master said, "He who aims to be a Noble Person does not seek in his food to gratify his appetite, nor does he seek in his dwelling place the appliances of ease: he is earnest in what he does, and careful in his speech; he frequents the company of persons of the Way that he may be rectified: such a person may be said indeed to love to learn."[1]

ANALECTS I:14

The Master said, "Learning without thought is labor lost;[2] thought without learning is perilous."[3]

ANALECTS II:15

4 A premise of Confucian learning is the self-recognition of faults. Learning must begin with each individual's recognition of his or her own need to engage in learning, of the faults within the self that must be overcome.

Similarly, religions often distinguish between what *is* the case and what *ought* to be the case in their appraisal of the condition of the world and humankind. Judeo-Christian traditions, for example, describe the foundational condition of humanity as one of religious alienation, or sin, a falling away from the proper relation with God, and they offer ways in which humankind might move back into the proper relation with the source of ultimate truth, God. The world *is* in a condition of religious alienation; it *ought* to transform itself toward a relation with God.

Confucius has also suggested that the state of the world is far from the ideal of the sages of antiquity. In this passage he brings the same perspective to the individual and states that he finds no examples of individuals who are willing to see the dichotomy of *is* and *ought* and who are willing to admit the limitations and errors of their condition, the *is*, in order to move toward what *ought* to be the case, the moral goodness embodied in the sages. How many of us today take refuge in the self-importance of the "I" and the "me" as they are, the *is*, instead of what we could or should become, the *ought*?

The Master said, "It is all over! I have not yet seen one who could perceive his faults, and inwardly accuse himself."[4]

ANALECTS V:26

5 To study with or under someone, it was necessary to present a gift, or tuition, if you will. In fact, it was a livelihood for many a teacher. A bundle of dried meat was one of the lowliest gifts that could be presented to a teacher, very different from the emoluments that could be offered by the rich. However, Confucius took in *anyone* as a student regardless of his background, wealth, or station in life.

With this statement, Confucius freed the process of learning from a mark of nobility by birth to one of nobility by moral virtue, a teaching he claimed as a direct model of the ways of the ancient sages. At the worldwide level in the time of Confucius there was no possibility of free access to education. If you think of the denial of access to education and learning because of race, gender, religion, wealth, or so many other distinctions, the issue seems as pressing today as it was in the time of Confucius. Who today would accommodate the student who can offer only a bundle of dried meat? You might say it is food for thought!

6 While Confucius may take on a student of any background, nonetheless he has high expectations of all his students and he is not an easy mentor! Confucius expects his students to be eager to learn, to take up the trials and tribulations of learning enthusiastically and with great energy.

7 This is a fundamental formula of intelligence that has long been quoted in Confucian circles as a standard for students. If Confucius holds up one corner of a problem, he says, he expects the student to come back with the other three. Quite a demanding standard! In Confucius' understanding of learning, answers are not handed out; information is not instantly available—learning is a long and demanding *process* in which information is internalized, reflected on, and examined. Even with the advanced tools we have at our disposal—the Internet, blogs, and search engines—we may fall far short of this very simple formula. How do we find the teacher in our day who demands of us three corners?

The Master said, "From the person bringing his bundle of dried meat *for my teaching* upwards I have never refused instruction to anyone."[5]

The Master said, "I do not open up the truth to one who is not eager *to get knowledge*, nor help out anyone who is not anxious to explain himself.[6] When I have presented one corner of a subject to any one, and he cannot from it learn the other three, I do not repeat my lesson."[7]

8 Learning never stops, even when walking with companions! Confucius turns this situation into one of learning by suggesting that we should always be aware of the possibilities for learning, and vigilant of both positive and negative sources in this learning process.

We, too, have companions with whom we walk; we, too, have our role models. Today's major "walking companion" might be the mass media, which tells us again and again that material things are important; "they are us," as they say, they are what is essential, true, and real. Is this manufactured image of reality, this collage of personas, to be emulated for what it *is*, or *ought* such creations to be avoided?

9 Confucius teaches us to always reach out to what is beyond our grasp, to strive for the *ought*, as you move beyond what *is*. Dive into learning with full commitment, for you should always think of the end point as being beyond your greatest efforts.

Perhaps in our own day it is difficult to think of a goal that is essentially unattainable. We are, after all, conditioned constantly to satisfy our goals in the here and now. Most religious traditions are little different from Confucius in suggesting the complexity, subtlety, and enormity of their ultimate goals. Patience, tenacity, and composure are necessary in the long journey toward self-understanding. We must trod the path that is set upon the goal, however distant. The famous Christian theologian Søren Kierkegaard referred to this step as the "leap of faith," something each person undertakes in his or her own fashion to keep on going, whatever the odds.

10 This passage stresses the need for extensive and broad learning. Such learning, when coupled with the following of propriety, will not miss the mark. The propriety component puts things in the right context of solemnity and seriousness, otherwise called *ching*, reverence.

Learning takes the whole of our heart and soul. It points us toward a higher idea, a goal of ultimate meaning, and because of that goal, it requires that we move beyond our normal concerns.

The Master said, "When I walk along with two others, they may serve as my teachers. I will select their good qualities and follow them, their bad qualities and avoid them."[8]

ANALECTS VII:21

The Master said, "Learn as if you could not reach your object, and were *always* fearing also lest you should lose it."[9]

ANALECTS VIII:17

The Master said, "By extensively studying all learning, and keeping himself under the restraint of the rules of propriety, *one* may thus likewise not err from what is right."[10]

ANALECTS XII:15

11 This is a follow-up to the earlier selection in *Analects* II:15. The vocabulary in this passage is the same, the relation of learning, *hsüeh*, to thought, *ssu*. Confucius suggests that he has engaged in a process he describes as "thought only," that is, just *ssu*, reasoning or reflecting, without learning accompanying it, while fasting and denying himself sleep. We seem to have a regimen of behaviors suggestive of contemplative or meditative practice.

It is presumed that this was undertaken precisely to understand the components of mental activity. For Confucius, however, thought, *ssu*, without learning is of no use and even less use when under the rigors of fasting and sleep deprivation. Learning was always seen as a plodding and difficult path where nothing could be simplified, nothing rendered easy in a moment of ecstatic or mystical experience. Only through the toils of learning, *k'un hsüeh*, and, as the great historian of religion Joachim Wach called it, a total commitment of the total person, could a person come to see the true character of the individual and thus fulfill her moral responsibility to others and the world in general.

The Master said, "I have been the whole day without eating, and the whole night without sleeping: occupied with thinking. It was no use. The better plan is to learn."[11]

ANALECTS XV:30

7 □ Truthfulness and Righteousness

The character for *hsin*, truthfulness or faithfulness, is composed of two parts: *jen*, the stand-alone character for "person," and *yen*, meaning "speech" or "to speak." When combined they literally mean "what one says" or "person speaking." How do we get from "person speaking" to "truthfulness" or "faithfulness"? Presupposing that what you say is in accord with the truth makes the connection. In the context of Confucian teachings, you speak from the foundation of the learning of the sages of antiquity, and therefore truthfully. "Faithfulness" is derived from the sense of the word *hsin* as not only speaking the truth but also fulfilling your commitment to it, as suggested by philosophers David Hall and Roger Ames in their rendering of *hsin* as "living up to one's word."

I, a far more complex character, is rendered most frequently in Confucian writings as righteousness or rightness. It is composed of the character *wo*, self, and a character that carries the connotation of goodness or beauty. The combination suggests "goodness within the self," or more specifically the individual's ability to reveal what is good. The connection is drawn between the inner quality of goodness and the outward expression of correctness, the visible display of righteousness or rightness cultivated through learning.

What I find interesting about both *hsin* and *i* is the degree to which they both reference an inward condition expressed externally. This relationship of inward and outward reinforces the nature of learning as something that transforms the individual. Confucius sees the degree to which the individual outwardly manifests the transforming inner nature as a critical measure of progress in the learning regimen.

1   A person who lacks truthfulness or faithfulness is not going to be trusted in any pursuit, just as animals cannot be utilized to pull a carriage without a yoke. So it is with a person: the yoke is the foundation of moral action. While the yoke conjures up for us an image of oppression, the point is not that it controls or restricts the individual, but that it provides a means to express what is within the individual.

2   The passage is important not only for the position given to *hsin*, truthfulness or faithfulness, but also for the grouping of four subjects that Confucius claims as the emphasis of his teachings: "culture," *wen*, the content of all learning both narrow and broad; *hsing*, "ethics," meaning actions or behavior; "commitment," *chung*, loyalty or giving yourself completely; and finally, *hsin*, the outward expression of inward moral cultivation. These terms describe the nature of the Noble Person as well as the products of the learning process. Do we expect that those who pursue learning will bear out the interior content of that learning?

3   See *Analects* II:13 (chapter 3).

Truthfulness or Faithfulness—*Hsin*
The Master said, "I do not know how a person without truthfulness is to get on. How can a large carriage be made to go without the crossbar for yoking the oxen to, or a small carriage without the arrangement for yoking the horses?"[1]

ANALECTS II:22

There were four things that the Master taught: culture, ethics, commitment, and truthfulness.[2]

ANALECTS VII:24

Tzu-kung[3] asked about government. The Master said, *"The requisites of government are* that there be sufficiency of food, sufficiency of military equipment, and the faith of the people in their ruler." Tzu-kung said, "If it cannot be helped, and one of these must be dispensed with, which of the three should be foregone first?" "The military equipment," said the Master. Tzu-kung *again* asked, "If it cannot be helped, and one of the remaining two must be dispensed with, which of them should be foregone?"

(continued on page 85)

4 Confucius summarizes the elements he regards as critical to the ability to govern a state: food, military forces, and the faith or trust, *hsin*, of the people. Food would be given up before faith with the belief that the trust of the people is the single most important element in the governance of the state.

In *Analects* XII:17 we find a passage that serves as a basic definition of government or governing. The passage reads, "To govern is to rectify." It is actually a pun; the words "govern" and "rectify" are both pronounced *cheng*. The character for "govern" is composed of two parts, the character *cheng*, rectify, and the character for "hand." To govern means that you push into effect (with your hand) the process of rectification, or you "effect rectification." The bottom line, of course, is the connection between government and rectification, moral rectification, and this definition becomes foundational to Confucius in his broader teachings of the path of the ancient sages. The ancient sages were, after all, rulers, and part of what Confucius looks to in the paradigms of virtue is their capacity to rule with and through moral virtue.

Do we demand that our own government be held together by the faith and trust we have placed in it? Where is even the possibility of trust and faith, when the foundation on which it exists, the learning of the self, is subsumed in the culture of material plenty?

The Master answered, "Part with the food. From of old, death has been the lot of all people; but if the people have no faith, there is no standing."[4]

ANALECTS XII:7

5 | Confucius reinforces the traditional codes of sacrifice, reaffirming that sacrifice is only to be carried out to your own ancestors, not someone else's. To carry out such a sacrifice would be improper because it would seek the approbation of others. Such an act is inappropriate; it lacks righteousness or rightness, *i*.

6 | Part of the performance of *i*, righteousness or rightness, is what we might call righteous indignation. We must try to right wrongs as we see them, not walk away in the face of moral transgressions. We might also describe this attitude as conscience, that voice within us that says certain things are just plain wrong.

Conscience tends to focus on your own actions; righteous indignation in turn focuses on others' actions. Both these terms reflect the outward display of inward moral training, the absorption and inculcation of the learning of the sages.

7 | One of the five major disciples of Confucius; associated with the transmission of his teachings.

8 | One of the sayings by a disciple instead of by Confucius, but given the status of Tzu-chang and the inclusion of the passage in the *Analects*, there is no doubt that the tradition has interpreted the passage as worthy of canonical status.

9 | The passage summarizes the virtues of the scholar, *shih*, one who pursues the path of learning and makes himself available for public life. The scholar must be willing to sacrifice for the common good, even if it means his own suffering or death. The next sentence draws the distinction between *i*, righteousness or rightness, and profit, and thus suggests that *i* represents the moral character as inimical to what is profitable.

Hsin and *i* both establish criteria to measure the progress of learning, and also a judgment on the actions of those who act upon their learning.

Righteousness—*I*

The Master said: "For a person to sacrifice to a spirit that does not belong to him is flattery.[5] To see what is right and not to do it is want of courage."[6]

ANALECTS II:24

Tzu-chang[7] said,[8] "The scholar, *trained for public duty*, seeing threatening danger, is prepared to sacrifice his life. When the opportunity of gain is presented to him, he thinks of righteousness. In sacrificing, his thoughts are reverential. In mourning, his thoughts are about the grief *that he should feel*. Such a man commands our approbation indeed."[9]

ANALECTS XIX:1

8 ☐ The Teaching of Goodness

Jen, goodness, occupies a central position in any discussion of the Confucian tradition. Its core meaning is in the relation of one person to another, something we might render as "person to person." It has also been translated as benevolence, compassion, kindness, altruism, humaneness, and love. Confucian *jen* suggests the ability of relationships to open us to ultimate meaning.

We find an interesting parallel to this idea in the work of the Jewish theologian Martin Buber. In *I and Thou*, he focuses on people's relationships to each other, to their environment, to their communities, and ultimately to God. For Buber, the world has become fractured by the way in which we relate to everything around us; we not only fail to understand ourselves and our brothers and sisters, but most important, we also fail to understand God. The problem is that we view others as *objects*: they are not whole, not complete, and in turn we are not whole or complete in our ability to relate to them. Buber names these failed and fractured relationships *I-It*; that is, the *I* relates to others, God, and ultimately to itself as an *It*.

However, Buber offers the possibility of seeing the world afresh, of seeing our relationships in a new way, no longer as *I-It*, but now as *I-Thou*. Buber argues that through this new relationship the individual can be made whole in relation to the ultimate source of meaning, God.

Strikingly, Confucius' idea of goodness is crafted and defined precisely in the establishment of a very particular type of moral relation. And this is exactly what Buber means by *I-Thou*. Only when the other is seen as a *Thou* does the wholeness of the person and in turn the wholeness of the self exist. It is in the relationship of *jen*, goodness, that you travel the path of the sage, that is, the path to understanding the Way of Heaven.

 1 Goodness is the necessary backdrop for whatever aspects of life you encounter. To persevere in the face of adversity, you must draw on strength of character, a sense of self, a sense of mission and purpose. Likewise, you need a point of self-definition and self-understanding in a world where it is all too easy to be swayed or carried away by pleasure. We should consider goodness as that mooring, that foundation.

Goodness is the inward foundation and goodness is the outward expression, a point marvelously summarized in an often-quoted phrase from this passage, *jen che an jen*, literally, "The person of *jen* rests in *jen*," or "The good rest in goodness." Rest, or peace, *an*, is found in the ultimate goodness, *jen*, of Heaven itself.

 2 You might think that the person of goodness has the capacity to love *all* others. Instead, Confucius suggests that hatred is an appropriate response to that which is contrary to the teachings of the sages (see also *Analects* XVII:24, chapter 3). Confucius does not offer unconditional love for all, but rather guidance by the principle of moral goodness. When moral goodness is the measure of things, the person of moral goodness is in the best position to judge how others rise or fall by that standard. What meets the standard of goodness is praised and emulated. What falls short is condemned but is also always viewed as capable of rectification. There is in Confucianism an eternal optimism in the capacity of humans to be transformed toward goodness.

The Master said, "Those who are without goodness cannot abide long either in a condition of poverty and hardship, or in a condition of enjoyment. The good rest in goodness: the wise desire goodness."[1]

The Master said, "It is only the good person who can love or who can hate others."[2]

3 Here is an affirmation of the power of goodness. To establish intention and direction toward that which is good is to establish a goal for
your life that overrides all distractions, all temptations, all behaviors
unfit of the teachings of the sages. There is an analogy here to the earlier autobiographical passage where Confucius discusses his commitment to learning at the age of fifteen (see *Analects* II:4, chapter 11).
He says of himself that he had "set his will upon learning." The term
translated as "set," *chih*, is the same term used in this passage. In the
autobiography, the term suggests the level of commitment, total commitment of the total person, to the goal of learning. Here, the meaning is similar and also suggests the seriousness and thoroughness of
the commitment itself—in this case, the person with total commitment
to goodness.

4 Confucius sets the conditions for "those who truly love goodness,"
and comments on the difficulty of finding a person solely focused on
goodness. To hate what is not good is a strong declaration, but it
matches the adoption of goodness as love, *hao*, suggesting the
antithesis of the state of total commitment in the embrace of goodness. For the person of goodness, there is nothing higher than goodness itself. The reason Confucius can make that statement is that
goodness, *jen*, is simply the nature of Heaven.

5 As challenging as it is to find a person truly committed to goodness,
nonetheless, if the commitment is made, the goal is within reach. The
strength of commitment is something that Confucius suggests can be
possessed by each person. All it takes, he says, is the strength to practice it for a single day.

The Master said, "If the will be set on goodness, there will be no practice of wickedness."[3]

ANALECTS IV:4

The Master said, "I have not seen a person who loved goodness, or one who hated what was not good. He who loved goodness, would esteem nothing above it. He who hated what is not good, would practice goodness in such a way that he would not allow anything that is not good to approach his person.[4] Is there one able for one day to apply his strength to goodness? I have not seen the case in which his strength would be insufficient. Should there possibly be any such case, I have not seen it."[5]

ANALECTS IV:6

6 See *Analects* II:13 (chapter 3).

7 The question posed by Confucius' disciple is an attempt, as we find in many of these passages, to arrive at a more precise understanding of the concept of goodness. Confucius' answer suggests that a person with such qualities would be nothing short of a sage, *sheng*, even one recognized as such by the ancient sages Yao and Shun. Such a person has entered into a special relation with others, defined in terms of moral goodness.

8 Confucius describes the exercise of goodness in the relation of one person to another, defined always in terms of a moral relation. As a person wishes to bring his own goals to fruition, so he helps others achieve their aspirations—a fulfillment of the circle represented by *I-Thou*.

9 "Art of goodness," *fang chih jen*, suggests the perfection of a way or an art to manifest this essential quality of goodness. It is the proximity of the one to the other that permits the development of goodness to begin with, and perhaps most important, it is the self that is the measure of the other. From the self to the other is a cardinal Confucian principle—you begin within and move outward. It is no different in this fundamental relationship. As you look within, thus you manifest without. As you perfect within, thus you perfect without. You learn on the basis of what is near or close at hand, *chin*, and on the basis of what is near, you extend to what is far.

Tzu-kung⁶ said, "Suppose the case of a person extensively conferring benefits on the people, and able to assist all, what would you say of that person? Might he be called a person of goodness?" The Master said, "Why speak only of goodness in connection with him? Must he not have the qualities of a sage? Even Yao and Shun were still solicitous about this.⁷ Now the person of goodness, wishing to be established himself, seeks also to establish others; wishing to be enlarged himself, he seeks also to enlarge others.⁸ To be able to judge *of others* by what is nigh *in ourselves*—this is called the art of goodness."⁹

ANALECTS VI:28

10 The Chinese, read literally, translates, "If I wish *jen*, then *jen* is here, it has arrived." The ready availability of *jen* offers several possible interpretations. On the one hand it is simply a matter of the availability of or access to the teachings of the sages of antiquity and the degree to which Confucius believes that the teaching of the sages can be summarized in the teaching of goodness. On the other hand, the nearness of *jen* could suggest the degree to which Confucius believes in, though does not state, the immanent nature of moral goodness. It is also potentially a similar statement to the previous passage where the term *chin*, near or close at hand, is also used to describe the inner workings of goodness. Though the argument for the internal nature of goodness must wait until the later Confucian teacher Mencius, in Mencius' view and certainly for later Neo-Confucian thinkers, there is no question but that moral goodness is an essential part of human nature itself, *hsing*.

The Master said, "Is goodness a thing remote? I wish to have goodness, and lo! goodness is at hand!"[10]

ANALECTS VII:29

11   Also known as Yen Hui, the most famous of Confucius' disciples and Confucius' own favorite. He is said to have perfected the virtue of goodness, *jen*, and is generally considered to be the most accomplished of Confucius' disciples in learning, *hsüeh*. Unfortunately, he died young and so was not able to fulfill what Confucius saw as his future as the transmitter of the learning of the sages.

12   Here "self," *chi*, is importantly described as a potential limitation of and deterrent to the development of goodness. The potential negative role ascribed to the self by Confucius is captured in the phrase "subdue self," *k'e chi*, where the self is seen as potentially contrary to goodness, and goodness is seen as the result of "subduing" some aspect of the self. By subduing the self and returning to propriety, *fu li*, you show propriety toward that which is above, and by so doing, realize your own highest character as well as the proper attitude toward others.

13   The answer is assumed in Yen Yüan's follow-up statement asking Confucius for instruction in the practice of goodness. Though Confucius instructs him, just as the teachings have been transmitted from the sages, still Yen Yüan must take up the practice of goodness himself.

14   The process of subduing the self involves restraining yourself in seeing, hearing, speaking, and behaving. Confucianism, too, has an *is* and an *ought*, and that distinction applies equally to the self and society. Though not drawing the distinctions made by other religious traditions for the existence of evil in the world, Confucianism also recognizes that the world and the self are less than perfect. Confucianism thus draws an existential picture necessitating change and transformation if moral goodness is to be achieved.

Yen Yüan[11] asked about goodness. The Master said, "To subdue one's self and return to propriety is goodness. If a person can for one day subdue himself and return to propriety, all under Heaven will ascribe goodness to him.[12] Is the practice of goodness from a person themselves or is it from others?"[13] Yen Yüan said, "I beg to ask the steps of that process." The Master replied, "Look not at what is contrary to propriety; listen not to what is contrary to propriety; speak not what is contrary to propriety; make no movement that is contrary to propriety." Yen Yüan *then* said, "Though I am deficient in intelligence and vigor, I will make it my business to practice this lesson."[14]

ANALECTS XII:1

15 See _Analects_ XII:4 (chapter 3).

16 The term Legge translates as "slow" can be rendered as cautious or deliberate, suggesting not difficulty in speaking, but great wariness in the responsibility of speaking with due attention to moral goodness.

17 The phrase "difficulty of doing," _wei chih nan_, suggests that once your actions are understood for the moral challenge they represent, then there is no possibility other than cautious and slow speech. To feel the difficulty, _nan_, of doing or carrying out your responsibilities is to understand the moral responsibility of your actions, _wei_.

Whatever goodness is, it is directly tied to a sense of gravity in undertaking responsibilities. Such moral responsibility is goodness itself, again described as the relationship of one person to another and captured by our analogy of _I-Thou_.

18 Confucius suggests that some things are more important than life itself, specifically the upholding of goodness. There is a long tradition in Confucianism of people standing on the basis of a moral decision, a stand of conscience and righteous indignation, enduring great suffering, including torture and death, in the name of upholding what is morally right. How many of us today are willing to pay such a price?

Ssu-ma Niu[15] asked about goodness. The Master said, "The person of goodness is cautious and slow[16] in his speech." "Cautious and slow in his speech!" said Niu. "Is this what is meant by goodness?" The Master said, "When a person feels the difficulty of doing, can he be other than cautious and slow in speaking?"[17]

ANALECTS XII:3

The Master said, "The determined scholar and the person of goodness will not seek to live at the expense of injuring their goodness. They will even sacrifice their lives to preserve their goodness complete."[18]

ANALECTS XV:8

19 See *Analects* XIX:1 (chapter 7).

20 Others have translated "gravity" as respectfulness, courtesy, and earnestness. "Generosity" has been translated as tolerance, breadth, and liberality. "Sincerity" is the only term we have seen in another context, *hsin*, truthfulness or faithfulness, and it has been translated as trustworthiness and good faith. "Earnestness" has been translated as quickness and diligence. Finally, "kindness" has been translated as generosity and clemency.

21 The definition of goodness is clarified in the examination of the results of the practice of each of the five virtues listed. In summary, a person of goodness is seen as a person trusted and respected, someone capable of winning the hearts and minds of everyone, and someone for whom others would gladly serve. As you practice goodness, so do others respond.

22 See *Analects* II:8 (chapter 4). Although this passage comes from Confucius' disciple Tzu-hsia rather than the Master himself, the fact that it is contained in the *Analects* suggests its canonical status for the tradition as a whole.

23 First, goodness is connected to broad learning, that is, not just the Classics, but also the relationships with others that make up the fulfillment of moral responsibilities. Second, goodness is manifest in the true commitment to learning, in pursuing the path of the sage and the Way of Heaven. Third, goodness is found when you proceed with earnestness, with total commitment on this path. And fourth, "reflecting with self-application," *chin ssu*, is literally to reflect on things at hand. You turn inward in examination, outward in reflection, but always on things that are near at hand.

"Reflections on things at hand" may be the best way to understand *jen*, goodness. What can be nearer than the relation of one person to another? And in the wholeness that is foundational to that core definition of person to person, we see the other as ourselves. We no longer view the world as *I-It*, but now as *I-Thou*, and in this mode we look for a way to express our manifestation of goodness as action.

Tzu-chang[19] asked Confucius about goodness. Confucius said, "To be able to practice five things everywhere under Heaven constitutes goodness." He begged to ask what they were and was told, "Gravity, generosity, sincerity, earnestness, and kindness.[20] If you are grave, you will not be treated with disrespect. If you are generous, you will win the people. If you are sincere, people will repose trust in you. If you are earnest, you will accomplish much. If you are kind, this will enable you to employ the service of others."[21]

ANALECTS XVII:6

Tzu-hsia[22] said, "Learning extensively and having a firm and sincere aim; inquiring with earnestness and reflecting with self-application: goodness is in such a course."[23]

ANALECTS XIX:6

9 □ The Single Thread

Confucius' teachings cover such a large spectrum that the manner in which they might be elucidated or illuminated can appear to be a wide and even divergent path. The disciples at times express the need to condense Confucius' rich multiplicity of teachings into a quintessential message. Among the passages are several attempts to bring this multiplicity together and deduce the most basic and most essential teachings. The passages take two forms. In one case, they concern what will be described as a single thread, *i-i-kuan-chih*, in the teachings. In the other case, they define what will become the most basic platform of moral teachings for all of the various separate teachings and ideas Confucius shares with disciple and ruler alike, the teachings of *chung* and *shu*, loyalty and reciprocity, and the statement of the Golden Rule.

With the understanding of the disciples clarified we are then in a better position ourselves to ask the same question with the long reach of history and inquire as to what this teaching means to each one of us and how we might ground ourselves in this essential wisdom.

1 Personal name for Tseng-tzu, a prominent disciple of Confucius credited with transmitting the Master's teachings, particularly the teaching of the single thread. He is also one of only four disciples referred to as *tzu*, Master, an indication of the respect with which he was held.

2 The Chinese term for Way is *tao*. Legge translates *tao* in this passage as "doctrine," a sense I believe to be too narrow and restrictive. Way, or *tao*, is used to encompass the totality of a worldview, and in this case the term is expansive in its inclusion of a range of teachings, ideas, and practices.

3 Confucius describes the essential point and underlying foundation of his teachings as *i-i-kuan-chih*, literally "the single thread" that runs through everything he believes. Confucius suggests that all his ideas and various teachings are ordered according to this principle.

4 The first virtue mentioned, *chung*, is usually translated as "loyalty." We might think of loyalty as a relation to others, either individuals or a country, an abiding and often unquestioned commitment. However, this is not exactly what Confucius means.

A literal translation of the character *chung* is "the heart or mind that hits the middle or mean," which suggests holding to a standard. A deeper meaning focuses the sense of "middle" or "mean" upon what is true to the self. Thus, Legge renders the term "to be true to the principles of our nature," which suggests the importance of self-reflection.

5 Like *chung*, loyalty, *shu*, or reciprocity, is also a critical part of the single thread. Composed of the character *ju*, meaning "to be like" or "similar," and the character *hsin*, "heart" or "mind,"*shu* literally means to be "like-hearted" or "like-minded." This phrase suggests that you put yourself in the position of other people, sharing their sorrows and joys with sympathy and empathy.

6 "This and nothing more" attests to the sense that *chung* and *shu* have thoroughly defined the "single thread" of Confucius' teachings.

The Master said, "Shen,[1] my Way[2] has a single thread[3] that runs through it all." The disciple Tseng-tzu replied, "Yes!" The Master went out, and the *other* disciples asked, "What do his words mean?" Tseng-tzu said, "The Way of our Master is loyalty[4] and reciprocity[5]—this and nothing more."[6]

ANALECTS IV:15

7 Personal name for Tzu-kung. See _Analects_ II:13 (chapter 3).

8 The disciples view Confucius as a person of extraordinary knowledge and intellectual capacity. However, Confucius is quick to gainsay this idea. It is not, he says, that he has extraordinary knowledge or memory, but that a single unifying principle runs throughout all his teachings. Confucius instructs his disciples to heed the overriding concerns, the unifying principles, and not just the superficial context of the teachings.

Ultimately, the issue is of depth, not just breadth. Knowledge can too easily be valued for its breadth, for its encompassing of a field, but Confucius calls us once again to look deeply inside ourselves, something we can too easily dismiss when breadth is our main concern.

9 This is the clearest enunciation by Confucius that the heart of his teachings is the revelation of _shu_, reciprocity, one word that brings all the teachings together.

10 Some five centuries before the Christian formulation of the Golden Rule in the gospel of Matthew, Confucius defines his most essential teaching by the very concept that most of us would easily recognize as our own quintessential religious and ethical heritage. A similar phrase occurs in _Analects_ XII:2.

Many interpretations have been given across the years about this parallel between Confucian and Christian ideas, including for some even Christian borrowing of the Confucian source. Others have sought to emphasize that while the Christian statement is in the positive, the Confucian utilizes negatives, i.e., do _not_ do to others what you do _not_ wish done to yourself. But such issues collapse in the sheer magnitude of the commonality of human expression outside of a historical and thus causal connection. The history of religions bears witness to a number of such articulations, all focused upon what Confucius would include in his teaching of reciprocity and Jesus might define by the Good Samaritan.

The Master said, "Tz'u,[7] you think, I suppose, that I am one who learns many things and keeps them in memory?" Tzu-kung replied, "Yes, but perhaps it is not so?" "No," was the answer; "I have a single thread that runs through it all."[8]

ANALECTS XV:2

Tzu-kung asked, "Is there not one word that may serve as a rule of practice for all of one's life?" The Master said, "Is not reciprocity[9] such a word? What you do not want done to yourself, do not do to others."[10]

ANALECTS XV:23

10 ☐ Reflections on Tradition

Several passages in the *Analects* relate directly to traditional Chinese religious practices, demonstrating the ways Confucius appears to criticize them. These passages have been used over the years to argue that Confucius' worldview is devoid of religious sentiment.

However, Confucius' questioning and interpretation of certain religious practices is not unlike the responses of a number of religious figures throughout history. After all, religions could never evolve or be created without key figures saying that something needed changing in the religious practices of their day. Christianity grew out of Judaism because of a series of challenges to the practices of the traditional Temple. In turn, Muhammad saw Christianity as deeply flawed in its understanding of the commands and nature of God and thus established a new scripture in the Qur'an. The position was new, yet built upon previous foundations.

Many have argued that Confucius shifted traditional religious beliefs toward a form of humanism centered on ethics, not religion. In fact, it is quite obvious that ethics is at the very heart of Confucian teachings, just as ethics is at the center of religious discourse historically and in our own day. There is no religious tradition that does not cultivate a code of ethical behavior to fulfill its religious teachings. Strangely, however, scholars do not say that the Buddha teaches us an ethical code, so he is an ethicist, not a religious figure.

If religion is, as we have suggested, the movement from what *is* the case to what *ought* to be the case, we must act in ethical ways that demonstrate that we are moving toward the highest ideals given to us by what we regard as ultimate.

1 Sacrifice was ubiquitous in the traditional Chinese religious world-view and was performed for the benefit, appeasement, or celebration of the spirits or supernatural beings, most commonly *tsu*, the ancestral spirits. It was assumed that sacrifice could establish the correct relation with the spirits, but only if the sacrifices were performed correctly. In this worldview, the spirits were unquestionably real.

Virtually all scholarship has assumed that in this passage Confucius is raising doubts about the *existence* of the spirits when he says you sacrifice "as if," *ju*, the spirits were present. However, I believe Confucius' main point is not to question the spirits' existence, but to ask what is most essential in sacrifice, and for Confucius the attitude accompanying the performance is most essential.

We don't *see*, *hear*, or *feel* the spirits and yet we conduct sacrifice. Suppose, however, we were actually to *sense* them, that is, to suppose they were actually present during the performance! Would their presence not produce the correct attitude precisely because they are *tsai*, present?

2 Perhaps this is an obvious observation, but when returned to the role of the spirits, the statement emphasizes Confucius' commitment to the attitude accompanying sacrifice. You sacrifice with a total commitment, the kind of commitment possible if the spirits were *actually* present, otherwise it is *as if* you were not even attending the sacrifice, which is no sacrifice at all!

As we have seen in the passages dealing with ritual and music, Confucius' focus is on developing and perfecting an attitude of *ching*, seriousness or reverence. By focusing on attitude and away from performance, Confucius has approached the traditional religious practice with a new and different perspective.

He sacrificed *to the dead,* as if they were present. He sacrificed to the spirits, as if the spirits were present.[1] The Master said, "I consider my not being present at the sacrifice, as if I did not sacrifice."[2]

ANALECTS III:12

3 One of the twenty-five disciples but not one of the ten prominent disciples.

4 This is one of the most frequently quoted statements purporting to demonstrate Confucius' disinterest with things *religious*. He insists that the world of human concerns and needs is of much greater importance than the world of the supernatural. Does this mean that he is not religious? Only if you define religion as focusing on the supernatural!

Confucius may simply be substituting one religious framework for another—the needs of humankind and the development of the moral character instead of supernatural concerns. That substitution does not *exclude* what is religious but *defines* it for him in a remarkably new and radical way.

5 Here is an interesting array of topics! But they represent substantial common ground in that all are out of the ordinary. Confucius is not interested in the bizarre or extraordinary in whatever form it takes. What he wants is learning and more learning and the development of the moral character in order to properly address the real needs of humankind.

Is it not a consistent trait of human nature that we dwell on the extraordinary, not the common? We seek the bizarre; we do not necessarily want to attend to the mundane needs of those around us. Here is a simple but poignant message: stay away from the distant and the exotic; focus on what is "near at hand," *chin ssu*—this should be the object of our study and actions.

Fan Ch'ih[3] asked what constituted wisdom. The Master said, "To give oneself earnestly to the duties due to humankind and, while respecting spiritual beings, to keep aloof from them, may be called wisdom."[4] He asked about goodness. The Master said, "The person of goodness makes the difficulty *to be overcome* his first business, and success only a subsequent consideration; this may be called goodness."

ANALECTS VI:20

"The subjects on which the Master did not talk were extraordinary things, feats of strength, disorder, and spiritual beings."[5]

ANALECTS VII:20

6 Another name for the prominent disciple Tzu-lu. See *Analects* VII:18 (chapter 2).

7 In contrast to traditional religious practices, Confucius again places first priority on serving human needs. As long as human needs have not been met, how can there be attention to the realm of the spirits? It is not a challenge to the existence of the spirits, but a prioritizing of human responsibilities.

8 Here is another statement that to some appears to demonstrate a lack of *religious* intent. To the question of the nature of death, Confucius quips that *life* itself is unknown and if this is the case, then *death* could not possibly be known.

Many have concluded that the question of the status and nature of death is fundamental to the nature of religion, and that if Confucius professes to know nothing of death then by definition he is not religious. But perhaps his answer presents an even greater mystery about and reverence for the state of death than were he to attempt to articulate something about it.

Chi-lu[6] asked about serving the spirits *of the dead*. The Master said, "While you are not able to serve humankind, how can you serve *their spirits?*"[7] *Chi Lu added*, "I venture to ask about death." He was answered, "While you do not know life, how can you know about death?"[8]

ANALECTS XI:11

11 □ The Way of Heaven

Confucius claims that he is a transmitter of the culture of the sages of antiquity, which reflects the traditional religious worldview. We noted that the word "sage," *sheng*, means "he who hears" and "he who manifests." When examined more closely, the ability of the sage to hear is explained as his ability to hear the Way of Heaven, *T'ien Tao*. In turn, the sage's ability to manifest suggests his ability to implement the Way of Heaven. Finally, we have suggested that the Classics represent the repository of the teachings of the sages and the record of the Way of Heaven, and thus the Classics are the scripture of the Confucian tradition.

To make this interpretation plausible, however, one element needs to be put in place: the source that Confucius himself regards as religious. Without this element Confucius is an *ethical* teacher, not a *religious* teacher. The answer to this question will be found in the understanding of *T'ien*, Heaven.

T'ien is generally interpreted as the high god of the Chou Dynasty. The term refers to the celestial sphere; today the character most commonly means "sky." It is not comparable to a Western notion of Heaven as a place where souls of the departed find a home. Rather, it is simply a reference to that which is above, but with the connotation of the authority of a greater power over all things.

Though Confucius is reluctant to discuss Heaven, he accepts its existence; that is, he *believes* in Heaven. Furthermore, Confucius regards it as the force behind the sages he seeks to emulate, as well as the teachings of the Classics he seeks to transmit. Being ethical, fulfilling the teachings of moral goodness, is grounded in the acceptance of the religious authority of Heaven itself, and Confucius is thereby a *religious* figure.

1 This is regarded as an autobiographical statement by Confucius. Most scholars have seen the passage as a commitment to the learning necessary to become a Noble Person. If we look at the passage as a religious autobiography, however, the emphasis changes from one of simply developing moral goodness through learning to one of understanding the religious implications of learning.

2 At fifty, Confucius understands what lies behind the learning of the sages that he has followed and advocated so strongly—what they have heard of the Way of Heaven, the final source of authority that gives meaning and purpose to life. And then, showing extraordinary humility, he says that he doesn't hear the Way of Heaven with a "listening ear" until he is sixty. How human! Even Confucius struggles with the intent to reach self-understanding. Only at the age of seventy can he say of his life that it is in complete accord with the Way of Heaven. Confucius has exemplified a religious life of increasing proximity and accord to the source of his own religious depth, the Way of Heaven.

The Master said, "At fifteen I had set my will upon learning.[1] At thirty, I stood firm. At forty, I had no doubts. At fifty, I knew the will of Heaven. At sixty, I heard it with a listening ear. At seventy, I could follow my heart's desires without overstepping what was right."[2]

ANALECTS II;4

3 A minister of the state of Wei with whom Confucius held conversations.

4 Apparently, this was a popular proverb of the time. The simplest interpretation suggests that the southwest corner of the house was understood as a location of comfort and security. By contrast, the furnace was said to represent an important location for the maintenance of the household, that is, conducting the business of the house. Thus the proverb appears to mean it is better to pay attention to your duties than to find your place of comfort and security. As such, it would seem to suggest you fulfill your responsibilities before seeking your due safety and comfort. In that respect it sounds rather Confucian!

5 Perhaps this was not the response expected! Confucius suggests that he places priority in that place of comfort and security rather than worrying about what is required to "maintain the household." If the foundation of security is established, then let the world come as it may; it can be met with equanimity.

Confucius' expression of the priority of comfort and security has its counterpart in our use of the term "faith." Confucius begins with the establishment of faith in Heaven. From that beginning point all else is secondary and all the practical details are covered. Faith does not mean a lack of knowledge but, as the historian of religion Frederick Streng has suggested, an acknowledgment of the relationship of the individual to what is ultimate,[3] in this case Heaven, and it is this relationship that Confucius prioritizes.

Wang-sun Chia[3] asked, "What is the meaning of the saying, 'It is better to pay court to the furnace than to the southwest corner'?"[4] The Master said, "Not so. He who offends against Heaven has none to whom he can pray."[5]

ANALECTS III:13

6 | See *Analects* II:13 (chapter 3).

7 | Nature, *hsing*, suggests the essential nature of a person at birth and thus is normally translated as human nature, though later Confucian tradition will question whether human nature is good at birth or whether goodness is accrued through learning. Confucius mentions the concept of human nature in only one other passage in the *Analects* (XVII:2) and without judgment as to its makeup.

8 | The list of subjects about which Confucius does not talk include not only human nature, *hsing*, but also the Way of Heaven, *T'ien Tao*. Confucius focuses on life, its character, the process of learning, and what can be described of its content and progress, not things beyond human description.

We should not conclude, however, that these exclusions suggest anything about disbelief in Heaven any more than they suggest that Confucius disregards the importance of human nature. Knowledge lies with silence in this case and poses another example of living with faith in Heaven, where faith is not so much a lack of knowledge as it is a relationship with that which is beyond description.

9 | An emissary and the minister of war in the state of Sung.

10 | Confucius ascribes the source of his *te*, virtue, directly to Heaven itself. The passage concerns a situation in which Confucius finds himself in some danger in his travels when threatened by a certain Huan T'ui. The story relates that this emissary wanted to kill the sage. Confucius' disciples wanted him to escape, but instead he is said to have responded with this statement, thus calming their fears.

This statement suggests Confucius' faith in the role of Heaven and in the purpose of his mission. There are several statements in the *Analects* in which we see Confucius suggesting that his role to restore the path of the sage is something he believes to be part of a larger purpose that ultimately finds its root in Heaven itself.

Tzu-kung[6] said, "The Master's views of culture and what was accessible may be heard. His discourses about nature[7] and the Way of Heaven cannot be heard."[8]

ANALECTS V:12

The Master said, "Heaven produced the virtue that is in me. Huan T'ui[9]—what can he do to me?"[10]

ANALECTS VII:22

11 Apparently a border town in the state of Chang.

12 Culture, *wen*, is identified as the teaching established by Chou Dynasty founder King Wen, which Confucius sees as the basis of his own transmission.

This passage finds Confucius in the state of K'uang and in some difficulty. The passage reaffirms even more strongly Confucius' sense of his own mission and direct connection to the heritage of King Wen. Given that Heaven invested King Wen with the Mandate of Heaven, the sanction of Heaven's rule, Confucius is saying that though he does not have the Mandate of Heaven, he has been charged with the transmission of the teachings of King Wen. Once again we have a strong sense of Confucius' faith in the role destiny has given him.

13 See *Analects* XII:1 (chapter 8).

14 This is a reference to the death of Confucius' favorite disciple, whom he felt had the greatest grasp of his teaching. We have seen that Confucius saw himself as fulfilling a mission granted him by Heaven. He seems here to extend that mission to the role he envisioned for his disciple, and now his disciple is gone. There is no doubt as to Confucius' level of grief and sorrow, and we can interpret Confucius' expression as one of crying out to Heaven in a moment of great loss.

But does he rail against Heaven as Job does against Yahweh? No. Does he express doubt in the existence of Heaven? No. Does he question the decision of Heaven that the allotted time of his disciple was too short? Not even that! Instead, Confucius' response is an acceptance grounded in his faith in Heaven, but also in his own sorrow.

The Master was put in fear in K'uang.[11] He said, "After the death of King Wen, was not the source of culture lodged here *in me?* If Heaven had wished to let this source of culture perish, then I, a future mortal, should not have had such a relation to that source. While Heaven does not let the source of culture perish, what can the people of K'uang do to me?"[12]

ANALECTS IX:5

When Yen Yüän[13] died, the Master said, "Alas, Heaven is destroying me! Heaven is destroying me!"[14]

ANALECTS XI:8

15 This pained statement shows Confucius' frustration that his teachings go unrecognized and that his devotion to learning and transmitting the path of the sage counts for little in the world. However, his learning does permit him to reach a deep and penetrating knowledge of the nature of things. This statement is unusual for Confucius, who seems always to admit the toils of his study and the great distance he must travel on the path of learning.

While there is no satisfaction from the response of humankind, there is comfort to be found in recognition for his efforts by Heaven—a comfort of greater magnitude than anything that could be provided by humankind. This statement articulates a sense of spiritual solace that lies beyond the reach of worldly understanding. A life without fame or fortune, while seemingly achieving little recognition, in the end achieves the ultimate form of recognition, to be known by Heaven. Is there any greater source of contentment and peace?

The Master said, "Alas! There is no one who knows me."
Tzu-kung said, "What do you mean by thus saying—
that no one knows you?" The Master replied, "I do not
murmur against Heaven. I do not grumble against
humankind. My studies lie low, and my penetration rises
high. But there is Heaven; that knows me!"[15]

ANALECTS XIV:37

16 Confucius seems to be comparing himself to Heaven, but we know that he was too humble to presume to do this. Commentators of this passage have instead suggested that the allusion to Heaven is to point out that you can understand Heaven not by listening to Heaven speak, but by watching Heaven's actions. In turn, Confucius suggests to his disciples that they ought to pay as much attention to his deeds as they do to his words: "Why can't you watch what I do, how I act, instead of always waiting for me to lecture to you?"

The understanding that all things are accomplished through Heaven is the very foundation of Confucius' faith. Much will be transformed as he transmits the teachings of the sages, but in this one respect, he is attempting to transmit what he believes the sages before him believed—that Heaven is the source of all things, all life, all activity, and all power for goodness in the universe. His role was to emulate this path toward the recognition of this source of ultimate meaning and to bring about ultimate transformation. This transformation is nothing short of moving from what *is* the case to what *ought* to be the case, a move that guarantees that he and each person he teaches can develop the potential for moral goodness that lies at the heart of the nature of Heaven itself. The essential yearning for moral goodness is what he believes the sages offered to humankind, and he therefore defines his teaching as the path of the sage, a path that brings each and every one of us and the world at large toward its ultimate meaning when bathed in the light of the Way of Heaven, *T'ien Tao*.

The Master said, "I would prefer not speaking." Tzu-
kung said, "If you, Master, do not speak, what shall we,
your disciples, have to record?" The Master said, "Does
Heaven speak? The four seasons pursue their courses,
and all things are *continually* being produced, *but* does
Heaven say anything?"[16]

ANALECTS XVII:19

12 □ Closing the *Analects*: Learning for the Self

The following passage provides an especially illuminating summary of the path of the sage for Confucius, as well as a road map for the continuation of our own paths. It introduces the term *wei chi*, literally translated as "learning for the self," a phrase that might at first glance seem quite antithetical to everything that Confucius' teaching appears to represent. After all, shouldn't learning be for others? Upon closer examination, however, the phrase has a rich and profound layering of meaning that leaves us anticipating further learning and reflection on the nature of these teachings.

1 The two key terms in the passage are *wei chi*, "for oneself," and *wei jen*, "for others."

Placing the self before others can have two quite different meanings, however, and the passage plays with these. On the one hand, learning for the self sounds like self-aggrandizement, the very antithesis of the teachings of the sages. Confucius criticizes the scholars of his own time precisely for such self-aggrandizement. Legge renders *wei jen*, "learning for others," as learning by the individual "with a view to the approbation of others," a rendering that insightfully draws our attention to the very issue that most concerns Confucius—that even learning is undertaken only for the pursuit of wealth, fame, position, and status.

On the other hand, learning for the self can be understood as part of the process of self-understanding. The learning of the ancients was indeed directed toward the self, that is, toward self-improvement, self-reflection, and self-understanding. This self-understanding in turn leads toward self-transformation, the movement from *is* to *ought*, and it is only at this level that learning has fulfilled its true potential.

Ultimately, learning is both of self and for self. But be wary, as the *Shih Ching, Book of Poetry*, suggests, for treading the line between *wei chi* and *wei jen* is like walking on thin ice! Confucius' concern is as relevant to us as it was in his own day.

Real learning, *hsüeh*, is not for the approbation of others and it never can be. It is the quiet reflection, the pained process of learning that never stops. It is the reciprocity shown to others in need. These are the things that bring us to true learning and the true definition of *wei chi*, learning for the self. The path of the sage, then, is a road map of self-reflection, self-examination, and self-understanding, through what Confucius refers to as *k'un hsüeh*, the "toils of learning" (*Analects* XVI:9), that we might then turn to the needs of others as the sages of antiquity ultimately illustrated for all of us in their pursuit of the Way of Heaven, *T'ien Tao*.

The Master said, "In ancient times, people learned with a view toward themselves. Nowadays, people learn with a view toward others."[1]

ANALECTS XIV:25

Acknowledgments □

Every book has a story about its own beginnings. This one is no exception. I was approached by SkyLight Paths Publishing to ask if I might be interested in working on a book introducing the religious and spiritual teachings of the *Analects* of Confucius. I jumped at the opportunity. For many years I have felt the need to bring my scholarly training and career to bear upon actual issues in the real world. The "ivory tower" of academia, particularly in the humanities, does no one any good unless it engages itself wholly and unconditionally in addressing the real problems each and every one of us face in our daily lives. We live in a world desperate to meet humankind's most basic needs, desperate indeed as we measure the possibilities for even our survival as a species!

In the end, it is about understanding yourself and understanding others. My interpretation of Confucius looks at the importance of both aspects in the learning process. Only by understanding both others and ourselves is there any chance of moving toward truly living in harmony and sharing the beauty of this world.

But now to the business of acknowledgments—those who have made the writing of this book so very meaningful and pleasurable. Lauren Hill of SkyLight Paths is simply a wonderful editor with whom to work. We have had an extraordinary working relationship in the creation of this manuscript. Her perceptive insights have posed questions that have only served to further elucidate the material beyond anything I would even have considered. It has been simply a great working relationship, that's all there is to it!

At the personal level, my life is not complete without my partner! My sounding board on all matters of thinking through the creation of a manuscript, whatever length, has been my life companion of forty years now, my Judith, without whom none of this work would ever have been possible. I like to think we have been there for each other all these years, but I think maybe she has been there a little more for me! A thank-you seems trivial in relation to the gift!

Last, I would be remiss if I did not describe the setting from which much of this manuscript has been written. As I said, every book has a story. I sit nearly 9,000 feet up at the end of a long four-wheel-drive road in an off-grid retreat. Here I am surrounded by both human history—the remains of a ghost town some hundred years old—and natural beauty— the view of multiple 14,000-foot peaks that fill our landscape and our windows. Such a place brings the rattle and the clatter of our normal lives to a stop—time becomes timeless. And here in this setting, in this still-ness, my thoughts can turn finally toward the real questions that make us truly human: the meaning of our own lives within the world that cradles us all.

RLT
Cat Gulch, Colorado

Notes ☐

1. Karl Jaspers, *Way to Wisdom*, trans. Ralph Manheim, 2nd ed. (New Haven: Yale University Press, 2003).
2. See Norman J. Girardot, *The Victorian Translation of China: James Legge's Oriental Pilgrimage* (Berkeley: University of California Press, 2002).
3. See Frederick J. Streng, *Understanding Religious Life* (Belmont, Calif.: Wadsworth, 1985).

Suggestions for Further Reading ☐

Berthrong, John H. *Transformations of the Confucian Way*. Boulder, Colo.: Westview Press, 1998.

Buber, Martin. *I and Thou*. Reprint, New York: Collier Books, 1987.

Chan, Wing-tsit. *Reflections on Things at Hand: The Neo-Confucian Anthology Compiled by Chu Hsi and Lü Tsu-ch'ien*. New York: Columbia University Press, 1967.

———. *A Source Book in Chinese Philosophy*. Princeton, N.J.: Princeton University Press, 1963.

De Bary, Wm. Theodore, Donald Keene, George Tanabe, and Paul Varley, eds. *Sources of Japanese Tradition*. 2nd ed. New York: Columbia University Press, 2001.

De Bary, Wm. Theodore, and Irene Bloom, comps. *Sources of Chinese Tradition*. Vol. 1, *From Earliest Times to 1600*. 2nd ed. New York: Columbia University Press, 1999.

Fung Yu-lan. *A History of Chinese Philosophy*. 2 vols. Princeton, N.J.: Princeton University Press, 1952.

Girardot, Norman J. *The Victorian Translation of China: James Legge's Oriental Pilgrimage*. Berkeley: University of California Press, 2002.

Hall, David L., and Roger T. Ames. *Thinking Through Confucius*. Albany: State University of New York Press, 1987.

Jaspers, Karl. *Way to Wisdom*. Translated by Ralph Manheim. 2nd ed. New Haven: Yale University Press, 2003.

Kieckhefer, Richard, and George D. Bond. *Sainthood: Its Manifestations in World Religions*. Berkeley: University of California Press, 1988.

Lau, D. C., trans. *Confucius: The Analects (Lun yü)*. London: Penguin, 1979.

———. *Mencius*. London: Penguin, 1970.

Legge, James, trans. *The Chinese Classics*. 5 vols. Reprint, Hong Kong: Hong Kong University Press, 1970.

Munro, Donald J. *The Concept of Man in Early China*. Stanford, Calif.: Stanford University Press, 1969.

Streng, Frederick J. *Understanding Religious Life*. Belmont, Calif.: Wadsworth, 1985.

Taylor, Rodney L. *The Confucian Way of Contemplation*. Columbia: University of South Carolina Press, 1988.

———. *The Illustrated Encyclopedia of Confucianism*. 2 vols. New York: Rosen, 2005.

———. *The Religious Dimensions of Confucianism*. Albany: State University of New York Press, 1990.

———. *The Way of Heaven: An Introduction to the Confucian Religious Life*. Leiden: E. J. Brill, 1986.

Taylor, Rodney L., and Frederick M. Denny. *The Holy Book in Comparative Perspective*. Columbia: University of South Carolina Press, 1985.

Tu Wei-ming. *Centrality and Commonality: An Essay on Confucian Religiousness*. Albany: State University of New York Press, 1989.

———. *Confucian Thought: Selfhood as Creative Transformation*. Albany: State University of New York Press, 1985.

———. *Humanity and Self-Cultivation: Essays in Confucian Thought*. Berkeley, Calif.: Asian Humanities Press, 1979.

———. *Way, Learning, and Politics: Essays on the Confucian Intellectual*. Albany: State University of New York Press, 1993.

Tu Wei-ming and Mary Evelyn Tucker. *Confucian Spirituality*. 2 vols. New York: Crossroad, 2004.

Waley, Arthur, trans. *Confucius: The Analects*. Reprint, New York: Alfred Knopf, 2000.

Watson, Burton, trans. *The Analects of Confucius*. New York: Columbia University Press, 2007.

———. *Early Chinese Literature*. New York: Columbia University Press, 1962.

Yao Xinzhong. *An Introduction to Confucianism*. Cambridge, U.K.: Cambridge University Press, 2000.

Index of Passages ☐

About SKYLIGHT PATHS Publishing

SkyLight Paths Publishing is creating a place where people of different spiritual traditions come together for challenge and inspiration, a place where we can help each other understand the mystery that lies at the heart of our existence.

Through spirituality, our religious beliefs are increasingly becoming a part of our lives—rather than *apart* from our lives. While many of us may be more interested than ever in spiritual growth, we may be less firmly planted in traditional religion. Yet, we do want to deepen our relationship to the sacred, to learn from our own as well as from other faith traditions, and to practice in new ways.

SkyLight Paths sees both believers and seekers as a community that increasingly transcends traditional boundaries of religion and denomination—people wanting to learn from each other, *walking together, finding the way.*

For your information and convenience, at the back of this book we have provided a list of other SkyLight Paths books you might find interesting and useful. They cover the following subjects:

Buddhism / Zen	Global Spiritual	Monasticism
Catholicism	Perspectives	Mysticism
Children's Books	Gnosticism	Poetry
Christianity	Hinduism /	Prayer
Comparative	Vedanta	Religious Etiquette
Religion	Inspiration	Retirement
Current Events	Islam / Sufism	Spiritual Biography
Earth-Based	Judaism	Spiritual Direction
Spirituality	Kabbalah	Spirituality
Enneagram	Meditation	Women's Interest
	Midrash Fiction	Worship

Printed in the USA
CPSIA information can be obtained
at www.ICGtesting.com
JSHW082336140824
68134JS00020B/1705